*Last of the
Hard Hat Divers 2*

Last of the Hard Hat Divers 2

BOB SINCLAIR

Self Published By Bob Sinclair 2011

Books by the same Author

Last of the Hard Hat Divers *(First General Release)*
Published by The Book Guild Publishing, Pavilion View 19, New Road Brighton BN1 1UF 2010
Copyright Bob Sinclair

Last of the Hard Hat Divers 2
Self Published by Bob Sinclair all rights reserved 2011
Copyright Bob Sinclair

ISBN 978-0-9568527-0-0

Acknowledgements

To my own dear Lady wife Mabe, for constructive critique which altered the original, without disturbing the truth of the narrative.

To Mr. David Robinson, the Literary Editor of the Scotsman Publications Ltd, for his guidance and advice so freely given.

To Captain Douglas Watt, who presented me with copies of original photographs which I had never seen, and which dated back more than thirty odd years.

And to Andy Young of the Scottish Sub-Aqua Club who also presented me with a photograph of myself diving forty years ago.

Printed and bound in the UK by CPI Antony Rowe, Chippenham and Eastbourne

Frontispiece

The Author about to be dropped into No 1 Caisson, Leith Docks (Original small photo was taken by my daughter Sheila in 1976)

Many years later it was converted into a full sized framed photograph and presented to me on the occasion of my official retirement in 1996 by Sheila.

Authors Update

To all my readers, mainly of the more gentle feminine gender, who were concerned enough to ask about the final fate of some of my old Buddy Divers.

I am happy to report that following the publication of my first book, I received word that many of my old Buddies among the Hard Hat Divers of my day are alive and well, for instance

NORTH SEA DIVERS Jack Sayers, Roger Lamplough, Geoffrey Kane and Peter Livingstone

FORTH BRIDGE CAISSONS Chief Diver Jim Sinclair and,

Troon Harbour Diver Paddy McCrory.

*This Book is dedicated to
The countless thousands who made a slight
mistake, and as a result, perished beneath an
unforgiving sea.*

Contents

1	Building the New Locks at Leith	11
2	Leith Docks Commission	19
3	Nash Dredging	28
4	Foreword to the Birthing of Bobsin	42
5	The Birthing of Bobsin	45
6	Spud Murphy's last Dive	54
7	The Big Blow	62
8	The Dead Man's Brake	70
9	MV East Shore	75
10	Jonathan	82
11	The Iguana Ranger	89
12	Of Rope and Smithereens	95
13	Jonathan Decorator	104
14	The Suicide	114
15	The Leg	120
16	A Clean Sweep	130
17	Martin's New Helmet	135
18	The Chippers	143
19	Gibson Heirs Foreman	156
20	The Yo-Yo	164
21	The Yellow Valve	174
22	The Deep Water Buoy	190
23	The Old Dock	200

24	Silted Brandy	212
25	Captain Wallace	221
26	Jonathan the Terrible	229
27	Brandy Galore	238
28	Lightships Granton	251
29	Pixie and the White Stuff	260
30	The Death of Cousin Dod	273

Chapter 1

Building The New Locks at Leith

After the Cockenize job finished I was pretty sure my diving career was over, I could have joined Jack Sayers and Tony Sparrow on the North Sea Oil Rigs but that would have meant I would be away from home indefinitely and my wife Mabel said she could not stand the continual worry. I could understand her feelings, for almost every week we would read about the endless procession of diving fatalities on the Rigs. They could not all be blamed on cowboy divers, although a large percentage of them were just that. I suspected the most likely root cause was untrained linesmen, probably coupled with too short decompression times for the depths they were working in.

I had tried applying for different Civil Engineering Projects, for instance the new Tay Bridge and although originally promised the work, it went to Fox Diving in the end. I also tried for the diving work on Balfour Beattie's intake and outfall tunnels for the newly built Power Station at Cockenize, but cousin Dod Donaldson and Ian Crow already had that job. The Agent of the Longannet Power station told me no firm would take on a single diver any more and since I had lost my long standing Buddy, Sandy McGill, I was now a single diver.

I spent the next three years as a Foreman Joiner, a Section Foreman and a charge hand Joiner respectively. The latter was with Edmund Nuttall on the sea bed, inside a huge cellular Dam which had been constructed to build the New Lock entrance to the Port of Leith. We were a small squad of only four joiners, my young brother Dickie Sinclair, who worked mates with our cousin, Terry Donaldson, who was Dod's young brother, Jimmy Archibald and myself.

We were employed building the extreme South East end of the new locks, including the massive culvert through which the harbour water would one day flow to raise the water inside the locks from the sea level outside, to the harbour level inside. I did not know at that time just how useful my knowledge of the whole complex system would be in the immediate future, once I resumed diving again.

Of approximately one hundred and fifty other men employed inside the dam, consisting of joiners, steel fixers, lorry drivers, concrete squads, crane drivers, Batching plant operators and small train drivers, I was surprised to find I knew only one man. That man was a charge hand joiner and a hard hat diver like myself. It was no other than my good friend Stevie Fox himself.

On our very first day on the job we found we had to go about our work wading endlessly through a thickish brown sludge midway up to our knees, which extended over the whole area of the former seabed inside the Dam. This was a mixture of sea water leaking through the cellular piles combined with mud, rotting fish, sea weed and shellfish which had perished when the whole area had been dewatered to allow the work to begin.

That first day at dinner time we had to climb a set of wooden stairs to reach the Canteen which stood on a Platform that kept it above the sludge level. As we climbed the stairs I saw Stevie Fox standing just outside the Canteen door. I immediately recognised his sturdy body and larger than usual head topped with thick, wavy black hair.
"Well Hello Steve," I said "what's this then, no underwater work?"
"Hi! Bobby, no, I have finished with the diving for good."
"Don't tell me you failed your Medical, like Big Sandy."
"No, I had no trouble with the Medical, it was my wife who made me give it up, she reckoned it was far too dangerous. She worked herself up into a lather over all those deaths out on the rigs and nagged me until I could take no more, so I packed it in, what about yourself, did you fail the medical?"
"No, physically I am alright, but I can't get any work on my own, now that I have lost my mate big Sandy. Mabel does not like me diving either, although she only tries half heartedly to stop me."

While we were talking, a shangi tractor and trailer pulled up at the foot of the stairs, on board were large urns filled with coffee and tea and literally dozens of tin mugs in open boxes. We were almost knocked off our feet as a crowd of men came pouring out of the Canteen as if it was on fire. They rushed down the stairs and began grabbing mugs and frantically trying to join the queues forming at the urns.
"Is it always like this at mealtimes?" I asked Steve.

"Yes, you see the last men get mugs spattered with sludge and very little time left of their half hour meal break, I bring a flask with me rather than join that bunch."
"You mean that sludge is here all the time?"
"Yes, they only sand bag and clear the area they are going to concrete that day, so the sludge pumps just pump it over the sand bags."
"They don't bring in any Queen Lizzie dump trucks to get rid of it permanently?"
"No way, that would cost too much" Steve said shaking his head:

A few weeks went by and it became one of the worst jobs I had ever been on. The smell of the sludge, containing the rotting fish, seaweed and dead shellfish became overpowering, I actually felt a sense of relief when my young brother told me he could take no more.
"Terry and I are packing up" he said,
"but I got a start for four of us, if you and Jimmy want to come with us?"
"What's the job?"
"It's with Token Construction renewing the whole of the old Leith Kirkgate," he said then laughed out loud.
"What's so funny?" I asked,
"Oh! I was just thinking, if you do come with us, it will be the first job you and I will ever work on together, without you being my foreman."
Jimmy Archibald and I were more than glad to go with them and get clear of that horrible stinking sludge, so the four of us finished up on the Friday night. On Monday morning we arrived on the new job with our toolboxes and

Dickie left us to climb the stairs and report to the Foreman in his Office, he came back and said to me,
"The Foreman wants to see you."
"What does he want with me?"
"I don't know, I was giving him our names when he said, "Your brother, Bobby Sinclair, is he also a diver?" I said yes and he said "Oh! Send him up to see me."

I climbed the stairs to the Foreman's Office and on entering, shook hands with a very good friend of mine, Alastair McDonald. He was a man who had worked under me on two contracts where I had been his Foreman shortly after I had demobbed from the Royal Navy. Damn me if he did not immediately offer me a chargehand joiner's job, which, the money being good, I readily accepted, to the pretended disgust of my brother, for now I was his foreman once again.

About two months after we left the New Locks job, one of the small trains inside the cellular Cofferdam was pulling a flat back wagon along the rails, loaded with a skip of concrete weighing about three tons. The train was towing it along the levelled off sea bed when without warning the skip toppled off the wagon and fell on a man walking alongside the track in the same direction, killing him instantly. He was the only man to be killed on that job and his name was Stevie Fox, another old Hard Hat man had gone to meet his maker.

Strange the way fate can work at times, because Steve's wife thought diving was too dangerous, she had persuaded him to give it up. Now the poor lady was a widow due to a freak accident. Edmund Nuttall's Agent and staff ran a series of tests, whereby the little train was loaded with a similar skip of concrete and ran back and forth at varying speeds for a whole afternoon and not once did it show any sign of tipping.

Three months later, the Kirkgate job was almost complete when I received a message saying my Dad wanted to see me. We arranged to meet that night in my local bar the Speedway Arms on Marionville road. At that time my father worked for Young and Leslie Stevedores, in Leith Docks as a rigger, maintaining all the gear used by the Dockers.

That evening we settled ourselves with a rum and peppermint and a pint of Skol lager each. Dad then said,
"Spud Murphy came round to my shed and told me he had failed his diving Medical and would not be allowed to dive again, so the Leith Docks Commission are looking for another diver."
"What was the trouble, same again I suppose, high blood pressure?"
"That's right," dad agreed,"they are going to transfer him on to one of the tugs as a crew member. He also told me he spoke to the Port Engineer, Mr. Godden and put your name forward, so the job is yours if you want it."
"I want it right enough, did he say how I go about it?"
"Yes he said I should let him know and he will arrange an interview for you with Mr. Godden."
"Good, Oh! that's great dad, you go ahead and do that for me."

At my subsequent interview I found Mr. Godden, the Port Engineer, to be a very tall, quietly spoken Irishman, obviously very intelligent. He asked the most pertinent questions of me, to quickly gauge my underwater abilities. I answered yes, I could use underwater air tools, yes, I could weld and burn underwater and yes, I did hold a Firearms Certificate and could handle explosives. No, I would require a medical, since my Fitness Register had not been signed for over three years. He then told me the job was mine provided I pass the medical and I was cleared by the C.I.D. as a fit and responsible person to be in charge of an explosive magazine. I then requested I be allowed time to resign my present occupation, to leave my job cleanly and with no rancour. Mr Godden granted this, saying he found this type of loyalty refreshingly commendable and so began my career with the Leith Docks Commission.

Dr Gordon Batters signed my Register up to date and was also happy to hear that my big mate Sandy McGill was alive and well. The C.I.D. man arrived and I recognised him immediately, for we first met while both of us were serving in the Royal Navy. We spent an enjoyable afternoon reminiscing over our Navy days, after which his report cleared me as a trustworthy person to be in charge of an explosive magazine. Mr Godden did leave me with a bit of a puzzle at the end of my interview, when with no explanation, he told me Martin Bendicks, my fellow diver, was never to be allowed into the Company's explosive magazine at any time. I decided there and then I must find out why and although I realised I could not ask Martin himself, that was out of the question, I determined however, one way or the other I would find the answer.

Cellular Dam around the construction of the New Locks outside the entrance to the old Tidal Leith Docks (In the background) far left circa: 1966

Photo courtesy copy from Harbour Master's Office

Chapter 2

Leith Docks Commission

My first day in the new job consisted mainly of being introduced to people all around. I knew only Martin Bendicks, my buddy diver, and first thing in the morning he explained we had to report to the Works Manager, David Grieve and tell him what our job was on that particular day. We were not supposed to deviate from the fairly comprehensive lists of annual routine work drawn up originally by Mr. Godden, unless David Grieve had some other pressing work which he needed to send us to immediately. Whenever this would occur, the routine work was left in abeyance.

Martin knocked on David's office door, minutes after 8 o'clock on that first morning.
"Come in" came a voice from within and we both entered. David was sat behind his desk apparently writing something on paper before him. He was a small, stockily built man in his late fifties with a fairly thick crop of wavy greying hair, which stood up inches above his forehead. A neat but completely grey moustache adorned his upper lip.

"Uh Ha!" he said as he looked up for the first time and laid down his pen. Martin then made the introductions and David stood up and shook my hand.

"We are making an examination of the Rank's Mill berth today" said Martin.

"No no" said David, interrupting him,

"just eh! just get ready, but leave Bobby with me and eh! don't go until, until eh! I send Bobby over to you. I'll get a man to show eh! show Bobby where the diving hut is."

"It's alright David" I said,

"I know where the diving hut is."

"Fine fine" David said,

"you just, you just eh! carry on Martin and leave eh! leave Bobby with me."

Martin left and David had me read and then sign a paper stating that as a diver, I must be prepared to turn to, and dive at a moment's notice, in any emergency a ship or the Docks might have, over any 24 hour period. He explained the diving department constituted a Port service which must be readily available at all times. Before I left David's Office on that first morning he reiterated the exact last words Mr Godden had said at my interview.

"Now mind, mind now Bobby at no eh! no time must you eh! ever let Martin anywhere near your eh! explosives magazine."

"Is there a reason for that, that I should know about?" I asked. David gave a strange little half laugh and half giggle that intermingled with his words.

"Heh! Heh! you will find, hee hee out soon, eh! soon enough, ha ha for yourself."

Faint alarm bells were ringing in my mind as I wondered why no one would tell me why Martin was not to be allowed near the explosive magazine.

After leaving David's office I walked over to the building which housed all the diving equipment. It lay directly opposite the inshore end of the Albert Passageway swing bridge. I climbed four wooden steps up to the entrance and walked in the door.

It was like stepping back in time. The interior was very dark, having no windows at all and as my eyes adjusted to the gloom, I saw what resembled a Siebe Gorman museum. There were literally a dozen old fashioned hand pumps, eight of them single acting for shallow water work and four double acting, powered by four men for deep water work. At the back of this large building lay stacks of used diving suits piled up against the wall and in front of them were underwater telephone sets. Some of them quaint old Siebe Gorman originals and some getting progressively more modern, until my eyes settled on at least six sets of the very latest models.

There was no ceiling above me and the heavy rafters landed on wall plates on top of walls, so thick, they allowed row after row of Diving Helmets to be stacked on the wall head between the rafters. In the centre of the building a large drying room had been built, which could accommodate at least four diving dresses pitched upside down on their stretchers and originally dried overnight by gas heaters but now converted to electricity. On the floor close to the right wall was a collection of Siebe hand cranking detonating boxes, again varying from the very old to the most modern.

To my immediate left there stood a cabin as big as a

Liner's state room with a ship's circular ventilator built into the top of the door. I knocked and opened the door, instantly I knew why it had been so dark inside the main part of the building, for all four front windows gave their light directly into the cabin.

Martin was sitting in an armchair in front of a two bar electric fire, he had spectacles on his face and was reading a newspaper.
"Come in Bobby" he said,
"that is your armchair," he pointed to a similar chair to the one he sat in. The inference was clear to me straight away, Martin wanted his own space, with no overlapping, fine with me I thought.

The floor was covered with the very best of ship's cortisene linoleum and a large table and four chairs completed the furniture. On the table lay a Royal Naval Diving Manual and beside it a set of Admiralty Decompression Tables. I said,
"Martin I have seen all types of diving huts in my time but nothing like this, this is sheer luxury."
"You have to be comfortable during the time you are not underwater," he said, rising and folding away his newspaper. "but I have been waiting for you for over half an hour so we better get cracking and get down to the boat."

The boat lay alongside No 4 Outer Harbour with her crew aboard. I was introduced to the boatman Jimmy Robertson, the two linesmen, George Smiles and Andrew Imrie, incidentally the Uncle of the famous boxer Tom Imrie. George took the helm and we set off, out the Fairway and across the Western harbour to the wharves alongside Rank's Flour Mill. Arriving alongside the pier Martin said,

"Do you want to take this one?"

"Ok but you will have to fill me in with what the job is."

"George will drop a shot line with a search line made fast to it and all you do is swing around a half circle on the search line and make sure there are no obstructions on the bottom that could damage the hull of the next ship delivering grain to the Mill."

"That's fine, sounds straight forward," I said as the lads started dressing me in the gear.

"One last thing" I said,

"what depth of water can I expect?"

"Oh! With the tide almost full, around about forty five feet." said Martin. Although George was tugging the wrinkles out of my bib at the time, I was aware of the swift look he threw at Martin, I could not read anything into that quick glance, but I felt sure George was unhappy about something or other, and I vaguely suspected it had to do with the depth Martin had just given me.

On the ladder now and fully dressed, George placed the shot line in my hand and tapped the top of my helmet. I stepped off backwards and slowly sank. The visibility was excellent and I watched a shoal of sprats veering out of my way as I dropped. I had not been in a suit for more than three years but my ears behaved themselves and pop popped beautifully as they equalised the increasing pressure of my descent. I dropped quite quickly, thinking I was going down into around about forty feet or more of water.

Suddenly I smacked boots first into a morass of soft spongy material at only around thirty feet deep. Although I instantly gripped the shot line to stop myself going deeper into it, it was so unexpected I was up over the waist in the thick glue like substance in that split second before I gripped hold of the shot line, George came on the phone,

"Did you say something Bobby?" with my heart beating rapidly at the sudden shock, it was with difficulty I kept my voice steady as I answered him.

"No George, I may have grunted or something like that but I did not say anything." An idea was forming in my head as I watched the swirling cloud of haze slowly clearing from around me. So, I thought, this is how they treat a new man, then I remembered George's quick glance when Martin gave me the depth and I realised he did not approve of what Martin was doing to me.

The haze had completely cleared with the flow of the tide carrying it away from me and I could now see I was up over the waist in grain, obviously spillage from the ships supplying the Mill. It must have built up over a long time and then swelled into a thick porridge. I decided Martin would get no enjoyment out of the dirty trick he had played on me and with both arms free, I hung on to my shot line left handed, and used my right hand to depress my spindle valve and began inflating my suit.

The glue like substance gripped tenaciously, so much so, I found my helmet rising above my head before a horrible sucking noise came from my lower body and I began a slight rise within the disgusting mess. I released my spindle to vent the extra air but gripped the shot line about one foot higher as my helmet settled back on my shoulders. George came back on the phone and I realised he must have heard my first attempt to extricate myself.

"Is everything alright Bobby?"

"Fine George," I answered, there was no way I was going to ask George to haul me out bodily, and give Martin the satisfaction of hearing me call for help.

I depressed my spindle once more. This time it was not quite so noisy and I rose almost two feet before having to vent air again. I gripped the shot line higher and waited until my helmet settled back on my shoulders. I could now move my legs a little, so I swung my right boot around the shot line, in case my next attempt should make me too buoyant and send me soaring to the surface.

At last I came clear and looked down at myself, from my waist belt, including my holster and knife and down both legs and over my boots was a thick coating of that noisome mess.

"Ok George I am coming up" I said,
"I won't spindle up, I am too near the boat, so I will come back up the shot line, take up my lines slowly."

Once I was standing back on the ladder George took off my helmet. Martin had a look of disgust on his face as he looked at the glaur plastered on me and he quickly said.
"Don't come on board, the lads will try to clean you up where you are,"
"Like hell I won't come on board" I said angrily and I clambered into the diving cockpit. "I won't go into the cabin in this mess, I will sit in the stern sheets and you can get me out of this filthy gear NOW."

Martin did not argue with me and the lads broke me out of the suit without trying to clean up any of it, so the stern sheets were soon stinking with the rotten grain. I don't know whether Martin intended it as a test to see how I would react to it, or whether it was some kind of a sick joke but I realised the crew were unhappy with the resultant mess of the diving boat although they said nothing.

Once we arrived back at our own berth, Martin wasted no time and rushed off the boat up to the diving hut on his own. I stayed on board and gave the lads a hand to hose down and clean the cockpit of the boat, after they had thrown the filthy suit up on to the quay side. While we finished the cleaning up Andrew Imrie muttered,
"Stupid big German bastard."
"What do you mean German?" I asked.
"His father was German and I am pretty sure his mother was not married to him either."

We were by now sitting comfortably inside the boat's cabin and George stretched out on the bench seat opposite us and said,
"I thought that was right out of order, doing that to a new man on his first day on the job." I noticed our boatman, wee Jimmy Robertson cupping one hand behind his right ear, which had a large hearing aid curved around the back of it.
"I think he is just plain ignorant," said Jimmy.
"that must have given you a real fright Bobby, landing in that muck heap."

I had been one day in my new job and already I had learned there was no love lost between the diving team and Martin. I would soon find out he was a bit of a loner, preferring to be alone. He was also one of the most fastidious and eccentric men I ever met.

At dinner time he would head up to the hut and strip to the waist and wash all of his upper body in ice cold water, in the large sink just inside the diving hut door. He would do the same thing again when we finished each night and again first thing in the morning before we left our berth. I soon discovered he appeared to suffer from some form of repetitive cleaning syndrome whereby he constantly kept sweeping out our cabin, emptying the ash trays, picking up the tiniest scraps of paper or anything at all that fell to the floor in the diving hut, which he kept highly polished and scrupulously clean at all times.

Then once more he would return to washing his upper body, cleaning his teeth, grooming his pencil mustache and plucking small hairs from his nose and ears endlessly. If the old saying "Cleanliness is next to Godliness" is true, then Martin Bendicks must stand desperately close to the Great Architect of the Universe himself.

The Author brings the Diving Boat through old Leith Docks

(Photo courtesy of Captain Douglas Watt)

Chapter 3

Nash Dredging

One morning Martin and I stood outside David Grieve's office and as usual as soon as the 8 a.m. whistle blew, signalling the start of the working day, Martin knocked on the door and entered, I also looked around the door to show I was present. David sat head down and was apparently writing on some papers before him, he laid down his pen, looked up at Martin and said,
"Uh! Ha!"
"Today we are examining berths in the Imperial Dock, Davy," Martin said. I was astonished at David's reaction.
"Oh! NO you are NOT" he said loudly,
"You've to get eh!, get all your gear on eh! on your Barge and tie in with, with FIGGATE and Norman and eh! Norman and Arthur. YOU ARE GOING TO eh! to help Nash Dredging that's what."
"What is this Davy?" Martin asked as if he was offended.
"Is it hate the diver week again?"
David stood up from behind his desk and in a calmer voice he broke into his, by now familiar, laugh / talk style.

"Ho!Ho! nothing to do with, ha ha ha, eh! to do with hate the diver, hee hee, hate the diver week Martin, but you have to help, eh! help Nash Dredging until eh! until further notice."

Before leaving David's office, I did notice the scribbling actions of his pen across the papers on his desk, when we first entered, had left not one mark on the virgin white papers lying before him.

As we walked over to the diving hut, a misnomer if ever I ran across one, we could hear the loud groans and screeches of the GOLIATH dredger working out in the Forth and excavating the fairway approaches to Leith Harbour.

The steam tugboat Oxcar pulled alongside our quay, at No 4 Outer Harbour, towing our second craft, which was a 56 ton diving Barge. This was an old converted stone or mud carrying barge, complete with bottom doors, which could open up to discharge her cargo in deep water. Her hold had been partly decked over with wagon sole timbers and a deckhouse had been built on top to form an accommodation for our team and diving gear. In the centre of the deckhouse was an old coke burning bogey fire. It's chimney stack protruded well above the roof and when going full bore in wintertime, it fooled many people, who believed we had our own steam engine on board.

We climbed aboard the barge to find our crew had the diving pump running, with the storage tanks fully pressurised. Alongside of our barge lay the FIGGATE, the Commission's own echo sounder Launch and on board were her Skipper, Norman Morrison, an Outer Hebridean man and Arthur Robertson, a Shetlander same as my own father. Norman came aboard our barge and at last told us what the job was.

"For the last fortnight, Arthur and I have been following up behind the dredger GOLIATH and plotting a graph marking boulders on the bottom which are too big for the dredger to pick up, so Mr Godden decided to send out the Digger to lift them into stone barges and have them dumped at sea. Unfortunately the Digger's grab is not big enough for some of them, so you are being called in to sling them."

"They must be pretty big if the Digger's grab can't grip them." said Martin.

"Martin" Norman said, "some of them look massive on the graph and personally I don't think the Digger will have the ability to lift them at all."

"Oh!, come on Norman," said Martin, "the Digger can lift twenty tons or more on its inside purchase."

"Well wait until you see them," said Norman in his soft, quaintly hissing Hebridean Island's accent.

The tug Oxcar signalled she was ready to tow us out and Norman hurried away to his own boat. Our lads jumped ashore and let go our mooring ropes and we set off.

Although I had worked for a few months inside Edmund Nuttal's cellular dam, I had not realised just how far beyond the old Docks, the new locks were going to be.

We sailed alongside the old wooden West pier for what seemed like ages, before we cleared it and continued across the western harbour and past the cellular dam. All the way, the noise of GOLIATH was increasing.

She was an impressive sight, as we passed by her, an endless conveyor belt of huge phosphor bronze buckets descended into the depths and screamed and groaned as they tore their way through the seabed and returned fully loaded to the surface and were then carried horizontally over her bows to empty into her enormous hold, before continuing once again to descend into the depths in a never ending cycle. Each bucket looked big enough to scoop up our other wooden diving boat in one go. This had to be one of the Dutch firms biggest dredgers.

Some distance beyond the dredger lay our Digger at anchor. She was one of the largest floating cranes in her time. Nothing other than a very large pontoon which had a crane mounted at either end of her. One crane was short and rather dumpy, with two blocks mounted on it, the outer block for normal weights and the inner, with many sheaves for heavy lifts. At the opposite end of the Digger, the crane there, had a large grab hanging from it's hook.

An empty stone barge was moored alongside the Digger and bobbing close to it was an orange buoy, or stoy as it is called in Leith. The stoy was marking the position of a boulder to be cleared from the bottom, so we anchored the barge into the wind and fell backwards to pick up the stoy and make it fast to the diving ladder, as a make shift shot line, Martin then dressed and dropped down.

"On the bottom, Andrew" he said over the phone. Andrew poked out a tongue at the diver phone but depressed the speak switch at the same time and repeated,

"You are on the bottom Martin."

"Ok I am beside the rock Andrew, put Bobby on the phone."

"Put Bobby on the phone it is," Andrew replied, making a face at the box as he answered. I depressed the speak switch

"Right Martin you are beside the rock as you call it, what kind of rock is it and what size is it?"

"It's like a rugby ball in shape and it is higher than my helmet."

"Got that, what kind of rock is it, and is it sitting on hard standing?"

"It's sitting on hard standing right enough but it is just an ordinary rock."

"I mean what kind of rock is it, Sandstone, Granite, Whinstone or whatever?"

"It's just a plain rock," he answered in a tone of voice which sounded as if he was attempting to explain something to a child of limited intelligence.

Andrew, standing beside me listening, said sarcastically.

"You are wasting your time Bobby, he is so ignorant he won't be able to tell the difference between Whinstone rock and Blackpool rock."

I smiled, but thought to myself, 'I wonder what Martin has done in the past to cause the whole diving team to hate him so much.'

Martin then measured around the base of the boulder and gave us up the measurement. We married together some wire strops with shackles, to the overall length he required and sent it down to him. Martin passed the wire strops around the base of the boulder on the seabed and shackled them together to form a circle.

"Ok send down the crane" he said, and we lowered the crane hook, with a set of four leg chain brothers on it. Martin now hooked the four leg chains on to the base wire, equally spacing them around the boulder to form a rough basket.

"Get the crane man to just grip it and take it off the bottom and no more."

We repeated his orders and the crane man took the strain.

"Hold that," Martin called,

"right take up my lines, I am coming up, take me away."

"They should take you away right enough, you big bent nosed German bastard," said Andrew nastily, as he and George began retrieving the lines of their ascending diver.

Once safely back on board and divested of weights and helmet, Martin called to the crane driver to,

"Bring her up."

Steam hissed from the exhaust at the rear of the driver's cab and the rattling of the pistons signified the boulder was on its way up from the seabed. As the crane lifted it clear of the surface and swung around to deposit it in the stone barge, I could clearly see this was an igneous boulder, most probably thrown out of the volcano, eons of years ago, which today is the hill of 'Arthur's Seat.'

I was very relieved to see it safely down inside the stone barge because the circular base wire was straining hard with the weight. Boulders born of molten lava are extremely heavy. One boulder of that size was enough for the stone barge, so Oxcar took it in tow and set off out into the Firth of Forth, heading for deep water beyond Inchkeith island to dump it.

Bunty Watson, the Skipper of the digger, called his crew to man the steam winches and warp the digger over to a second stoy nearby. We lifted our own anchors and moored alongside the Digger as she came towards us. When we reached the stoy we took it on board our barge and made it fast to the diving ladder and Martin dressed again and went down. This time he reported a boulder similar in size and shape to the first one, so we gave him down the retrieved base wire and shackles.

Back on board after slinging the second boulder Martin called
"Bring her up." The crane man called across as he was heaving up,
"This one is quite a bit heavier than the last one." Fearing it might be too much for the base wire I called back to him,
"If it is heavier than the last one, keep it just below the surface until the tug comes back with the barge,"
"Ok" he answered. We settled down in the cabin for afternoon tea and biscuits and to await the return of the tug.

About twenty minutes later I came out of the cabin to stretch my legs and found the boulder high above the sea. I could see this one was quite markedly heavier than the first one, and I called over to the crane man sitting in his cabin.
"Why have you brought it up out of the water?"
"Because Bunty told me to bring it up."
Bunty was standing on deck, eating a sandwich and heard what was being said.
"What did you want it left in the water for?" he asked.
"Because it's lighter in the water and less of a strain on the base wire."
"Rubbish" said Bunty scornfully.
"how can it be lighter, just because it's in water."
I had been joined by George and Andrew and George said,
"That man is an old retired trawler Skipper from Newhaven and as dour as they come, you are wasting your time trying logic on him."

I saw the sense of George's words, so I said no more and returned to the cabin to await the return of the tug. Ten minutes later a sudden bang announced the base wire had gone and the boulder was back on the bottom. We rushed out to witness the crane jib whipping back and forth like the rod of some demented trout fisherman.

The Oxcar hove in sight and told us to suspend work for the rest of the day on orders from the Harbourmaster. We were told we must clear the fairway for shipping arriving shortly, so we set off back to our own berth, towed back by the tug and Martin said,
"I know you should be diving tomorrow but if you don't mind I would like to finish my job."
"That's ok by me Martin" I said, for I felt as Johnny new man I was not going to rock the boat this early on in our relationship.

Back at our berth, Martin climbed up on the quayside saying,
"I am going up to the diving hut but I will tell Jimmy Melville, the rigger, to put some heavier wire strops aboard us for tomorrow." then he turned and looked back at me.
"How can the boulder be lighter, just because its in water?" he asked. Feeling rather tired because of the ignorance surrounding me I answered
"Because it weighs less, by the weight of the water it has displaced."
He shook his head, in obvious disbelief of such a statement and was gone.

I had taken to staying aboard with the lads until fairly close to finishing time and then going up to the hut to fill in my daily diving diary. This was something I would carry out faithfully every working day, for the full eleven years I was with Martin:

The following morning the tug arrived to take us out first, then come back for the Digger, which had some problem or other to be fixed before leaving her berth. As we sailed out past the west pier, Martin was dressing in his woollens when he suddenly stopped George, just as the linesman was offering up the long drawers to his feet, and looking past George out of the barge's open door, he exclaimed
"What stoy is that on our foredeck?"
"That's the stoy that marked the position of the boulder we lost yesterday," George answered.
"What the hell did you bring it on board for?" Martin asked in an exasperated voice.
"Because Bobby told us to bring it on board after the crane man lifted the boulder," said Andrew. Martin looked accusingly at me and said,
"What the hell did you do that for, and how do you expect me to find the boulder without a marker stoy."
"I will land you on the boulder with our shot line" I answered.
 "Aye that will be right" Martin said,
"out in the middle of the Forth Estuary, you are going to place a shot line right on the boulder I was working on yesterday, George, have you ever heard anything so stupid in all of your life?" George, bless him, said
"He seems pretty sure he can do it Martin."

When the base wire broke the day before and the boulder returned to the bottom, I realised I had been too hasty in telling the lads to bring the stoy aboard, so I had taken bearings on the boulder's new position under the Digger at that time.

We were now coming close to the position we had been in the day before and I directed the Tug on to the line I wanted. The wind was blowing from the same direction as yesterday and we dropped two stern anchors and moved forward to set a fairly wide spread of another two anchors into the teeth of the wind. The Oxcar left us and headed back in to bring out the Digger. With Andrew's help I allowed the barge to drop off the wind and working with all four anchors, we brought her into the position I wanted and secured her around the bits.

While we were occupied in positioning the barge, we could hear the continuous harangue Martin kept up the whole time, while he was dressing inside the deckhouse.

"I will tell you now George, there is no way I am going down into fifty feet of water and searching around all over the place for a boulder which could be hundreds of yards away. I am not going into saturation diving just because somebody was silly enough to lift the marker before the job was complete."

I stood on the deck, holding the shot line, and checked my meads, or in other words my bearings. My father had taught me well and I scanned the far off shoreline, to make sure there was no mistake. With a three-point bearing I would expect to be reasonably close. With a five-point bearing I knew I could hit a kitchen table, smack on, be it two hundred feet below us. Satisfied with our position I fired the shot line over the side and secured it to the diving ladder.

Martin, fully dressed, slid off the ladder and sank below the surface, grumbling over the diver phone all the way down.

"George, after I have been searching for twenty minutes let me know, because that's all the time I am going to give it before coming back up."

"Right Martin got that, twenty minutes it is from now and you are coming back up."

"On the bottom George" Martin reported then said immediately,

"I don't believe this George, I am right beside the rock, talk about luck."

"Well Martin," George answered as he smiled and winked at me. "I don't know about luck, for Bobby seemed pretty sure he could land you right on it."

I do believe most of mankind's advances come from the handed down experiences of our humble ancestors. Without doubt the Archimedes, Newtons and Einsteins were the Giants who made great strides forward in science and mathematics, to the advantage of all humanity, yet the ordinary people of years gone by solved so many of their own problems, one way or the other, and handed down the amazing results to us.

My forbears fished the seas around the Shetland Isles from time immemorial, sometimes going as far as thirty or forty miles off shore to what they called the 'Far Haaf' (the open sea) and as long as they could still see the distant coastline, they had the ability to take meads or bearings and read the bottom perfectly. They could plot and find certain rock hazards and areas of sand between those rocks where it was safe to fish, without losing valuable gear they could not afford to lose.

One of my ancestors, who lived approximately 200 years ago, was a man called Gideon Sinclair. He was a bit of a rebel against any authority that held sway over the small crofting and fishing community he belonged to. He owned a large open fishing boat of the type called a 'Sixareen' crewed by six men who each had one share of the catch apiece. The 'Sixareen' was equipped with a lug sail and for most of the time they had plenty wind to take them to the fishing grounds, but on calm days six men would row the craft with a long heavy oar each. This was back breaking work, to pull such a heavy craft for thirty to forty odd miles out and at times back again and Gideon finally rebelled against the Church of Scotland's demand of a full share of the fish every time they came ashore.

He stated he did not mind the tithe of donating one day's full labour each man was obliged to give the Kirk per year, but he would be damned if he would give an eighth part of their fish every trip they made, they already had the extra burden of a seventh share to their Laird.

The minister removed him from the Church's Elder list and banned him and his family from the Kirk for life. He rowed across the voe (Bay) one Sunday and offered to make a deal with the Congregational Minister of a neighbouring Parish, whereby he would honour the tithe of a day's labour each year coupled with an occasional share of the boat's fish and this was promptly accepted by the Minister.

From that day onwards Gideon and his family would dress in their best clothes and row across the voe every Sunday to attend the Kirk there. His crew stood by him, for

Gideon had the rare ability to memorise all the bearings he **ever** took and knew the fishing grounds better than any other man.

He could also find the kelp forests, where line fishing was impossible due to the long tough fronds standing up from the sea bed more than ten feet high. They would rip these fronds out of the bottom with special claws they built for that purpose and bring them up more than two hundred feet, just to harvest the giant 'Yogues' which anchored themselves to the tough bases of the fronds.

Yogues, the Shetland name for enormous mussels, one of which, when opened, would fill a large soup plate with its meat. Now, with the Yogues, they had plenty bait for their hand lines and set lines and Gideon would shift their grounds, according to a new set of meads or bearings and fish the sea bed with a confidence born of countless years of collective experience. This then, was the knowledge my ancestors acquired and handed down, through the centuries directly to me.

The Digger duly arrived and using the heavier wire strops Jimmy Melville the rigger had put aboard us, Martin slung the boulder and the tug towed it away in the stone barge.

We were to continue this operation for many weeks on end with boulders of varying sizes found by the Figgate as she systematically plotted a graph over all the area excavated by the dredger Goliath. Her echo sounder determined which ones were deep enough and could be safely left alone and which ones must be removed. Then one day we came across one of the ones that Norman had spoken about. He was right, there was no chance that the Digger could ever lift one of these brutes.

Cellular Dam and Western Harbour to the Right

Courtesy copy from Harbour Masters Office.

Chapter 4

Foreword to The Birthing of Bobsin

Although she was in mid channel, the Mississippi paddle steamer had eased down to slow ahead. She was now approaching one of the most infamous areas to be found in all of the mighty river's long length. Here the currents were strong and completely unpredictable, the sandy river bed was forever being reshaped and moulded by the powerful waywardness of the currents, treacherous new shallows would form, where previously deep water prevailed.

The Captain was well aware of this danger of going aground, from the ship's bridge he called for a leadsman to take soundings of the bottom. On the foredeck a sailor appeared carrying a heaving line made fast to a long cylindrical lead weight. He walked forward and stepped on to a small platform which jutted out from the ship's starboard side, at her bow, he held the coils of the heaving line in the crook of his left arm while his right hand lowered the lead weight down to just above the surface of the river. All the way up the heaving line from the lead weight were pieces of different coloured bunting, sewn into the line at intervals of six feet.

A small group of passengers watched with interest as the leadsman began to swing the lead in a pendulum fashion. Skimming the surface, the weight swung back and forth higher and higher until it finally described a full circle above the leadsman's head, the sailor pulled hard on the line each time the weight passed over him and this increased the momentum of the lead and when he finally released his hold on the line, the weight sailed through the air in the direction the ship was travelling and plunged into the river. The sailor gathered in the slack line and as the ship passed vertically over the weight's position on the river bed, he noted the colour of the bunting at surface level and called out loudly, "BY THE MARK FOUR". This indicated four fathoms of water under the ship, or 24 feet. The sailor began recovering the lead weight from the river bed and prepared to repeat the procedure.

One of the passengers watching was an aspiring young author called Samuel Langhorne Clemens. The sailor once more called out loudly to his Captain, "BY THE MARK THREE," this was three fathoms or 18 feet below the ship. The young author was intrigued by the scene he was watching and moved forward to observe the swinging of the lead more closely, the sailor then sang out,
"BY THE MARK TWAIN," this was two fathoms or 12 feet of water under the ship. Samuel Langhorne Clemens smiled, for now he had his Nom de Plume (his name of the pen for his books to come.)

In a humble way I have one thing at least in common with the legendary giant of an author, who would come to be known as Mark Twain. For I had also heard a corrupted version of my name shouted aloud on board a ship as in the Birthing of Bobsin, and I had originally intended to use it as my nom de plume.

Chapter 5

The Birthing of Bobsin

I stood on the seabed and stared up at the rounded face of stone that towered above me. I paced around it and measured approximately 65 feet circumference. Phew! I thought, almost 22 feet in diameter, I pulled our shot weight alongside of it and using it as a counterbalance, I inflated my suit and rose slowly off the bottom until my helmet was level with the top of the boulder, now using the shot weight as an anchor, I remained there slightly buoyant and said.
"George, read my depth gauge" over the diver phone,
"Checking the depth it is," said George.
"you are 38 feet deep at the moment." I let my air spill and eased back down to the bottom and lay down flat beside the boulder.
"Ok George read it again."
"You are now 51 feet deep," George answered.
"Right George make a note of this."
"Give me a minute until I grab a pen and paper."
    Still lying on the bottom, I marvelled at the clarity of the sea water, now that we were well clear of the docks and

their silt, coming from the water of Leith river. Close to my helmet and anchored to a small flat stone was a sea anemone. I watched its waving tentacles and its ever changing hues of rich colour coming and going in an attractive, deadly display and I also watched its own little lure fish, as they swam fearlessly in and around the mass of the seeking tentacles.

A tiny minnow of a fish appeared in view and with fins vibrating very fast, it hovered above the anemone, watching the little lure fish sporting themselves around the inside of the miniature technicolour jungle. With a flick of its tail, the little fish turned and looked straight in my front light at me. It's tiny eyes goggled fearlessly into my own.

"Ready to write, fire away." said George.
"It is a blue whinstone boulder, around 20 odd feet in diameter and 13 feet high, so you can rest assured George the Digger won't be lifting this one either, mark it down on the chart as the biggest one so far."
"Got that Bob, will do," George answered.

My attention returned to the sea anemone. The tiny fish had lost interest in me and once more flicked around to watch the little lure fish joyfully rubbing side on through the waving tentacles. It must have been too much for the poor little fish, for he suddenly darted in to join the fun and was instantly grabbed by first one tentacle, then another and slowly but surely, many of them wrapped around him and carried him inwards, towards the maw of the waiting mouth.

I shook my head at the tragic little drama I had just witnessed, and wondered how evolution ever managed to bring about a relationship, such as a carnivorous, fish eating plant which would never ever harm its own little lure fish.

This was the fourth, and by far the biggest of the boulders we had examined to date, all of them beyond the lifting capacity of the Digger. I had already given David Grieve a written report on the first three, so it came as no surprise when I was summoned to a meeting with Mr Godden. On entering his office the following morning, I found a tall, slimly built and very well dressed gentleman was also present. Mr Godden introduced us saying,

"This is Mr De Vries, the general manager of the Dutch firm Nash Dredging. He is responsible for ensuring our Port will be capable of taking deep sea Liners in the future by deepening our approaches from the West, and this is Bob Sinclair, our diver and explosives man."

After the polite, 'Pleased to meet you,' exchanges were over, the discussion turned to the obstacles posed by the oversized boulders the dredger had exposed.

"Ve haff to remove ver fast so dredger not stopping." said Mr De Vries.

"you make 'em smaller by boom boom with the dynamites, so dredger can pick up, yes."

"Yes" I agreed,

"but some of them are pretty big and will take a lot of boring before we can split them with explosives."

"No no Bobsin" the Dutchman said, in an alarmed tone of voice,

"no bore, take long time, bore take long long too much, we need, how you say, bang-bang on top."

"You mean plaster charging with pannier bags on top." He smiled, obviously very happy with that method.

"Yes, iss much faster, much more boom-booms done quicker." I looked at Mr Godden, he said nothing, merely raising his eyebrows questioningly. I said,
"That will take an awful lot of detonators, cordtex, pentonite primaries and submarine gelatin dynamite and be dreadfully uneconomical."
"Bobsin" said the Dutchman almost hysterically,
"iss nothings to cost of dredger eh! Mr Godden." My Boss nodded in agreement and said.
"We will do it Mr De Vries's way, just order up whatever you need and Mr Grieve will get it for you." The meeting at an end Mr Godden escorted me to the door saying quietly,
"Remember Bob, on no account must you ever allow Martin Bendicks anywhere near your magazine." I would have loved to ask him why, but he closed the door behind me.

We started off destroying some of the smaller of the oversized boulders first, and of necessity, I stayed on board and made up the charges and Martin placed them in position. Being within a half mile of Ranks Flour Mill, I deliberately kept the shots down to between ten and fifteen pounds of gelignite at a time, loaded into two pannier bags and hung on top of the boulder. Cordtex detonating fuse led from the charge up to the diving barge.

Once Martin was back on board and stripping off his gear, I would set and secure a detonator to the end of the cordtex and lower it over the side. The tug would then tow us out of harms way, while I paid out the electrical wires attached to the detonator, by unwinding them from a large drum.

For safety reasons the detonating box itself was never connected to the drum of electrical wires until the last possible minute. We would now ask the Harbour Master's permission to fire at a given time. When granted, I would connect the detonating box to the drum of wires and a quick up and down with the handle of the plunger, and hey-presto, fresh fish for supper.

Martin would dress again and go down for a look, if successful, the Digger would be brought out to lift away what she could and any other debris would be left for the return of the dredger, which was now at work deepening the whole of the Western Harbour.

On the day of the near disaster, our barge was moored alongside the Digger and we were over the top of the real brute of a boulder I had examined a fortnight previously. A charge of 15 pounds had been placed and with Martin back on board, Bunty had his men man the winches and heave away on the stern anchors to pull us and the Digger clear of the danger area. The Figgate came alongside and Mr De Vries climbed on board the Digger. A safe distance away and with permission to fire, I set off the charge.

Mr De Vries came aboard our barge, just as Martin left the surface to look at the result. Martin came on the phone and his first words were most unfortunate,
"You have hardly touched it" he said.
"other than a few small cracks across its top, it looks like nothing happened at all." Mr De Vries heard him and for a moment I thought he was about to have an apoplectic fit.
"BOBSIN" he screamed at me, "PUT IN PLENTY DYNAMITES," I tried to placate him saying quietly,
"Mr De Vries, we are less than half a mile from Ranks Flour Mill and Henry Robbs shipyard and only a quarter of a mile

from the Docks, I don't dare fire any bigger shots than that." The Dutchman proved that in a rage he had a far better command of English than usual, although he used some words it might have been much better not to have learned at all as he roared at me.

"BOBSIN, I don't care if you BLOW THE WHOLE FUCKING PORT UP, PUT IN PLENTY DYNAMITES." I tried once more to calm him down by saying,

"I will increase the charges, if you can get me permission to do so, from both Mr Godden and the Harbourmaster."

"I phone Mr Godden now" he said and rushed away, to climb aboard the tug Oxcar.

He was back within ten minutes.

"The harbour man say, see Mr Godden, he decide, and Mr Godden say you fire 50 pounds."

"FIFTY pounds!," I exclaimed, in horror, and I too climbed aboard the tug, to telephone Mr Godden and confirm he was in agreement.

Against my own better judgement, I made up a charge of fifty pounds and Martin placed it. I called to Bunty to haul us clear and he had his men man the winches once more. After a while, running backwards, Bunty shouted

"How bloody far back do you want us to go for God's sake." I ignored him and he waited only a very short time after that, as we carried on moving away from the area of the charge, then he had his men stop heaving.

"We are going back no further." he called over to me.

"Well you will be here all night" I answered,

"for there is no way I am going to set this lot off until we are a lot further back than this."

It looked like the proverbial Mexican stand off once more, for he was a stubborn old bugger, the two of us stood silently glaring at each other across the deck of the Digger, until Mr De Vries appeared from the tug's accommodation and said something to Bunty.
"Right lads" the dour old skipper shouted out,
"heave away aft and when we run out of rope up forward just throw the last of the anchor ropes over the side." The stupid man was not fooling me, I could see the lads up forward surging the Manilla mooring ropes around the bits. They had plenty of rope coiled at their feet, more than enough for the distance I wanted to go back.

At last I called a halt and in due course, I fired the charge. Lord God, every port glass aboard the Digger disintegrated instantly, as did all of our barge's Georgian wired glass windows. The Digger lifted about three or four feet and moments later came a real BANG and the Digger reacted as if she was bouncing down some gigantic staircase.
I prayed silently that her old hull was still sound, I felt I would never live it down if I had managed to sink her.

The reports started coming in. All the windows had gone in Henry Robbs welding sheds, the western gables of these sheds ran down into the sea. At dinner time that day one member of the Digger's crew had missed his passage with us and was left on the quayside, in front of the flour Mill. He had fallen asleep in his car. He reported that Ranks Mill shook violently as did the timber wharf his car was on. The Harbourmaster, Douglas Gray, was convinced we had blown ourselves up. The fish came up in their thousands, some of them with their swim bladders blown clean out through their mouths.

George leapt into our dinghy and made off after a dead seal, floating about a quarter of a mile away. He came back towing it and using the diving barge's own derrick, soon had it slung and brought up to deck level. It was a grey seal and appeared not to have a mark on it, its large dark brown eyes were open and gave the effect it was still alive. George began skinning it, and then we could see it was smashed to pulp internally.

Very few people realise just how powerful a shock wave can be generated from even a very small amount of submarine gelatin dynamite set off 50 feet deep, never mind a whole 50 pounds. Within half an hour I received a message from Mr Godden instructing me to revert back to my former strength of explosive charges.

Shortly after that near disaster, Mr De Vries called Martin and I aside, to speak to us privately.
"Bobsin" he said,
"Martin and you come to work for me, earn plenty big monies. We go every where's harbours, you do nothing but Boom Boom every where's and every days and Goliath dredger pick up, you earn plenty." Martin and I declined his kind offer to work for him and as we walked away I said,
"I have to go to court tomorrow so you are diving on your own," Martin laughed, displaying a set of natural teeth that shone with a brilliant whiteness.
"I think I will manage" he said,
"I was diving on my own for the first ten years in this job, long before the law was changed and made firms employ two divers or more on every job. Oh! by the way, why does that De Vries man call you Bobsin?"

"When I first met him in Godden's office, the boss introduced me as Bob Sinclair, it seems he picked it up all wrong and decided that after my birthing, I was named Bobsin Clair.

Chapter 6

Spud Murphy's last Dive

It was 2 o'clock in the afternoon on a Wednesday when we got the call to stop work on the Imperial Dry Dock gates and come back to the Tug berth lie, in the Albert Dock. We had been recalled to clear a fouled cooling water intake on the Tug the Craigleith. More often than not, the intakes were found to be blocked by the newly invented plastic bag material, especially the heavy duty variety, so we were fairly sure what the job would entail. As we were sailing back to the Albert Dock, Martin began telling me all about the special job we had scheduled for tomorrow and Friday.

"In the corner of the south Imperial cross berth, about six feet up from the bottom, are three water intake tunnels, which supply the Imperial Chemical Industries factory. The one built for them by W. and J. R. Watson on the land reclaimed from the sea, and they use the water with sulphur to make Sulphuric Acid."

Martin then began using his right forefinger as a pencil or a pen and began sketching a completely invisible drawing on the compressor room bulkhead, invisible to us, but apparently not to Martin.

"This is the shape of the metal grid, which is bolted to the face of the quay wall. We have to unbolt it and have it lifted away by crane, so we can enter the tunnels and travel in towards the factory. Our job is to clear the walls and roofs of the tunnels by scraping away the mussels and other marine growth, then air lift out all the silt that gathers in their bottoms every two years or so. It's an outside contract, so we get paid double money and double dives for it."

His eyes took on a wistful look and he actually sighed.
"They used to get us to do it over a weekend and that meant the money was doubled up again but Grievsie stopped us working on it on Saturdays and Sundays."
"Would you like to work the weekend on it, instead of tomorrow and Friday?" I asked. Martin turned his head and stared blankly at George, then at Jimmy and finally Andrew before saying to me testily.
"I just told you, there is no way Grievsie will let us work on it at weekends."
"Maybe I could talk him into it."
"You haven't a hope in hell, Bobby, believe me."
"Suppose he agrees, is everybody prepared to turn out."
"We will all turn out," Andrew said,
"it's the best paying job we have ever had."
"George" said Martin,
 "what would you make of him, he just can't be told."
"Still no harm in him trying I suppose," said George.

By this time we had arrived alongside the Craigleith and we tied up to the tug.
Martin remained in the cabin preparing to dress and make the dive. I looked in the cabin at him and said,

55

"While you are getting dressed I will take Andrew over with me to see David and ask him about the weekend."

Andrew and I crossed over the tug's deck, to climb up on the quayside and as we did so Martin shouted after us,

"Can you not take a telling, you are wasting your time, there is no way Grievsie will agree to us working on that job over the weekend ever again."

As Andrew and I approached the offices I said.

"When we get to his office I want you to go in first and don't say a word, even if he speaks to you, don't answer him, let me do the talking."

In that first year with the Leith Docks Commission, I had come to know and understand the nature of our Works Manager very well. David was a proper gentleman at heart but had a very soft streak in him, which he tried to cover up with his blustering manner. A soft sob story would reduce him to tears, but he would try to offset this, with a stubborn determination to oppose everything asked of him by his labour force.

Because of all the routine work Mr. Godden had mapped out for us annually, I realised David disliked the fact that most of the time Martin would tell him what each day's diving was going to be and he appeared to resent this apparent reversal of roles and I felt sure this was the reason he was so intolerant of us divers.

I knocked on his office door,

"Come in," he called. I opened the door and ushered Andrew in first, then followed in behind him. David's eyes were cast down and his pen was making a determined attempt to put some sort of mark on the papers before him.

"Ah Ha" he exclaimed, as he laid down the pen and looked up for the first time, straight at Andrew, then, obviously instantly confused, he quickly switched his gaze to me.
"What can I do for you?" he asked.
"David" I said,
"when I first started in this job you told me, as a diver I must always be prepared to work, whenever called upon to do so."
"That's right" he quickly broke in on me,
"and you eh! you signed the agreement to eh! the agreement to stand by that."
His eyes jumped back and forth rapidly between Andrew and I.

"I know that David, but to let you understand, George Smiles and I go trout fishing every Saturday with my father but these I. C. I . people want us to do their job over the weekend, now David, we are prepared to work as late as it takes tonight and all tomorrow and tomorrow night and the same on Friday, if you want us to, so long as we have the Saturday off to go fishing with my Dad."

I knew this would sound like a challenge to David's authority and I also had Andrew standing there as a witness to all that was being said. David quickly stood up behind his desk and said
"Ho ho ho now, ---Bobby son, you eh! you signed that, hee hee hee, you signed that agreement and you eh! have to eh! have to stand by it. You will, hee hee hee, have plenty of eh! plenty of other Saturdays to go eh! to go fishing with your Dad. I am sorry son but you will have to eh! you will have to give your fishing up eh! your fishing up this week."

57

Looking suitably disappointed, I said in a disgruntled voice, "So is that it then David, I must work, is there no more to be said"
"No more eh! no more to be said son"
I shook my head and turned to leave his office with Andrew.
"Sorry about that son," David called after me.
"you will have plenty other eh! plenty other Saturdays to go fishing with your dad."
This was David at his best, so sympathetic towards me but, oh! so firm regardless.

As we walked back to the tug Andrew said.
"Bobby I can hardly believe that happened."
"Human nature Andrew, he won't allow anyone to dictate to him, and because he thought I was trying to get out of working the weekend, he made me agree I had to turn out and give up my fishing trip, now Andrew, we must not say a word about how that was done to anybody, for it could be used again in the future, maybe even on the same job."
As we climbed on the tug's gunnel to board the diving boat, we could see the bubbles breaking on the surface above the cooling water inlet. I jumped aboard and walked into the cabin to find **Martin** peering out of the cabin's windows, confused, I again looked at the bubbles alongside the tug saying.
"Who is that down there?" Martin raised a forefinger to his lips,
"Shoosh" he said,
"it's Spud Murphy, he wanted one last dive in the gear for old times sake."

"You are taking a bit of a chance Martin, after all Spud failed his medical."

"So what, he told me it's a terrible feeling you get, when you realise you can never dive again, so when he asked me if he could take the dive I said o.k.."

Satisfied there was nobody in authority on the deck of the tug above us, Martin turned away from the windows and sat down.

"I know how I would feel if a doctor told me I would never dive again," he said and for the first time I caught a glimpse of a softer side to Martin's temperament. The concerned look was there, if only for a few seconds and then it was gone in a flash.

"Well" he said arrogantly,

"how did you get on with Grievsie. I TOLD you he would never agree to us working over the weekend, didn't I."

"We are working this weekend." Andrew said quietly.

"Oh! That's great," George said,

"I could do with the extra cash this week."

Since we came back on board, not one word had come over the diver phone. Spud was obviously well aware that he could not know who might be standing on the deck of the tug above us and within earshot of the phone.

The hiss of the air entering the helmet and the gurgling of the bubbles leaving it, were the only sounds we heard, then almost in a whisper, Spud said.

"Is it ok to come aboard?" George moved to the phone,

"All clear, you can come up." The diver came up the ladder and without stopping to have his helmet and weights removed he stepped inboard and entered the cabin and sat down on the dressing stool. George and Andrew took his gear off, while Jimmy poured out a cup of coffee to revive him. Spud did look a little weary, for after all, a standard hard hat man has to hang on to a belly line slung under a ship in order to work in mid water, otherwise he would fall to the bottom.

"I really enjoyed that" Spud said winking at me.
"You fooled the hell out of me, I got a bit of a shock when I came in the cabin and found Martin in here."
That last fling proved to be Spud's final dive and he was none the worse for it and he quite happily returned to his work, as a member of the tug's crew.

The following morning I was almost late for my work, as the car refused to start, to begin with. As a result I was some distance away from Martin when the whistle blew. I saw him knock on David Grieve's office door and open it and look around the door. I stopped dead in astonishment at the tirade that came out of Martin's mouth as he roared.
"See you, ya bastard, YA POT BELLIED little RAT you, you, SLIMY UNDERHAND SNAKE that's what you are.
You can stick your diving job right up your ARSE for all I care." and with that he slammed the door shut with such force I thought all the office windows must shatter.

He flew past me and I had to run to catch him up.
"My God Martin" I gasped,
"what the hell has happened?" I drew abreast of him and I could see he was grinning from ear to ear and damn me if he did not wink at me as well. He uttered not one word, until we entered the diving hut and then he collapsed laughing on his chair and said,

"On my way in this morning I met Grievsie heading for the main offices and he said to me, "just carry on as usual Martin, because I will be in Mr Godden's office for eh! for a long time this morning."

Martin rolled about in his armchair laughing so hard that tears ran down his face.

"I only waited outside his office for you to arrive." He could hardly continue as he giggled and wiped his eyes with a handkerchief.

"I saw that nosy bastard Jock Wallace, the sawyer, peeping round the Machine shop door." Once again he had to stop and give way to uncontrollable mirth.

"He sticks his neb in everywhere and has to know everybody's business so he can pass it on as gossip to the joiners and carpenters, so I thought I would give him a bit of real gossip to give to them."

"You mean the Office was empty," I said, following the thread of his story. He could not answer but nodded his head furiously and laughed and wept and wiped his eyes again. I too found this hilarious and laughed with him at the very idea of it, poor Jock I thought and I wondered if it might cure him of his gossiping.

I was now seeing another facet in Martin's temperament that I could relate to, he had a sense of humour similar to my own and although Martin was much older than I was, in fact he was only one year younger than my own Mother, yet already we were forging an affinity with each other.

Chapter 7

The Big Blow

"Do you think I could get the Commission to get me a new helmet?" Martin asked, I looked at his helmet, lying under his coiled lines in the cockpit of the boat.
"Why, what's the matter with it?"
"Its pretty beat up and well dented don't you think, and anyway, I have worn it for the last twelve years."
"What about all the helmets on top of the wall head in the hut?" I asked.
"I would not touch one of those, they have lain there since the beginning of the war." George handed me a cup of coffee saying,
"I think you should ask for a new one Martin, tell them your old one is worn out."
"Right" said Martin determinedly,
"I'm going up to see Grievsie right now."
   As soon as Martin left the boat, Andrew said.
"I thought divers always grow more attached to their helmets, the longer they have them."
"Andrew" said George,

"normal divers grow attached to their helmets." Our boatman Jimmy Robertson giggled and spilt his coffee over his legs.

"Are you superstitious Bobby?" Andrew asked.

"Not in the least," I replied,

"why do you ask, Andrew?"

"See that helmet of yours," he said, pointing out of the cabin at my helmet lying on top of my coiled lines.

"What about it?" I asked.

"That's the helmet Jimmy Ward died in ten years ago," he said.

"Were you with him on that day Andrew?" I asked.

"Yes, I was his linesman," Andrew said shaking his head sadly,

"he had decided not to take a diver phone with us, so we could do nothing to help him, after he failed to respond to our hand signals."

"Andrew," I said sympathetically,

"the whole tragic incident had nothing to do with you, it was Jimmy's decision not to take a phone and it was Jimmy who failed to check behind the gates for a boil of water before going down." Andrew showed his teeth in a tight grimace, saying through them bitterly.

"It was supposed to be Bendicks doing the job that day, I will never understand why Godden decided to send Jimmy instead."

"You asked me if I was superstitious Andrew, well Sandy McGill and I were diving with Balfour Beattie that day and we were told to cross the Forth to Kirkcaldy to assist in Jimmy's rescue. We actually set off and started the crossing only to be recalled and told that Royal Naval divers were already there.

A fortnight later my wife and I went into Burtons, the tailors in Leith street, so I could be measured for a new suit. The tailor took all my measurements and then said.
"The last time I measured a man on a Wednesday, same as today, he had almost identical measurements to yours, that man was a deep sea diver and he was killed two days later."

He walked away to get some material for me to look at, but as he did so I said.
"Yes, I knew him, his name was Jimmy Ward and like him, I too am a deep sea diver." My wife Mabel panicked and grabbed hold of my arm and tried to pull me out of the shop saying,
"Come on Bobby, we will try somewhere else." I stayed where I was, because Mabel and I are complete opposites in everything and she is very superstitious, no Andrew, I am not in the slightest superstitious."
"If its meant for you, it will not go past you," wee Jimmy said philosophically.
"Bendicks has had a few near misses" George said,
"but always got away with it."
"That's my point George," Andrew said,
"the big arrogant German bastard has the luck of the devil."

This conversation was getting very interesting to me so I said.
"Bendicks has had a few near misses George, such as?" George thought for a moment.
"Two years ago we were sent to examine the Albert passageway lock, which was losing water. Martin went down without checking behind the gates, he did not have a

phone either, his bubbles suddenly stopped and we could get no answer to our hand signals."

"What do you mean his bubbles suddenly stopped?" I asked.

"I mean we could no longer see them on the surface and it was a Dockhead man walking by who shouted down to us,

"Do you know your diver is up on the surface on the other side of the gates."

"We had to get a crane with a man help platform slung from it to lift him ashore."

"How in the name of God did he ever manage to get on the OTHER side of the lock gates?" I asked incredulously.

"Because he is the luckiest bastard in the world." Andrew interrupted nastily.

"Because" George said,

"the sluice paddle was completely rotten and part of it was missing, causing the blow of water. Bendicks was carried off his feet and his helmet smashed right through the rest of it, which gave way and he was blown clean through the gates to the other side."

"Oh! MY GOD" I exclaimed,

"he would have been crushed to death if the rest of that paddle had held."

"Now you see what I mean," Andrew said bitterly,

"he survived, and a good man like Jimmy was killed doing his job."

"That's a bit unfair Andrew," I said.

"that decision came from Mr Godden and not Martin."

"Bobby" Andrew said,

"even as a man, he is a failure, he could not manage to get his wife Martha pregnant, they have no bairns."

"Andrew" I said,
"there are many divers all over the world who were unable to have children, and many, many more who could only produce daughters."
"I never heard that one before." Andrew said thoughtfully, "right enough" his face cleared,
"when I think about it, Jimmy Ward had six daughters, what do you have yourself Bobby."
"I have five lovely girls, Hazel, Sheila, Fiona, Rosslyn and Pamela."

The conversation stopped abruptly when Martin jumped aboard saying,
"We have a job on."
"At this time" George complained, "it's four o'clock"
"We have to go, it's an emergency, Edmund Nuttal's cofferdam has sprung a leak."

I naturally thought it was the cellular dam he meant, but no, when we arrived there, we were turned back to the Imperial Dock and after locking in we discovered it was a three sided small dam. The fourth side being the north quayside of the Imperial Dock itself.

We moored to the quay, and Martin began dressing, while I went ashore to see the general foreman and take a look inside the dam. A huge pump was running at full bore on the inside, this was the biggest single pump I had ever set eyes on, it's delivery hose was fully two feet in diameter. It's output was prodigious and poured over the head of the small dam into the Dock and yet the water level inside the dam was holding steady at eight feet below the harbour level, with a most powerful boil showing on the surface inside the dam, some leak I thought.

I spoke to the General Foreman and explained I would require the huge pump to be shut off before the diver went down. I explained I would give his men a shout when Martin was ready, so as soon as Martin stepped on the ladder I called "SHUT THE PUMP DOWN." and to my surprise Martin turned his head and shouted angrily,
"Leave the pump running."
By this time George had begun roping up Martin's front and back weights and he looked over at me with a quizzical look on his face.
"George" I said quietly,
"he must not be allowed to go below with that pump running." Martin glared up at me then said,
"George, I am the man diving, you do what I tell you, not him, put my helmet on."

George picked up the helmet and made as if to pass it over Martin's head.
"George" I said,
"remember the rule, give the diver everything he wants except death." Poor George stood frozen, completely undecided and again Martin said forcefully,
"Put my helmet on George." Andrew spoke up for the first time.
"George, there is nothing worse can happen to a linesman than bringing up his diver dead." George said nothing but laid the helmet back down on the deck.

The stand off carried on for fully twenty minutes. Now I was seeing for myself just how arrogant and inflexible Martin could be. He stood there on the ladder resting his elbows on the top of the stringers with his head bowed.

The General Foreman came over to the quayside and called down to the boat,

"When is your diver going down?" Martin turned to face him.

"Just as soon as that man standing beside you stops interfering and lets me get on with my work." he shouted, then he turned back to George.

"Are you going to put that helmet on me?" I could not believe this was happening. He had not even looked inside the Dam.

"George" I said,

"there is an eight foot differential between the Dock level and the water level inside the dam and a really big boil on the surface on the inside. It only took a ten foot differential to kill JimmyWard."

"That's the truth for I was there," Andrew then confirmed what I had just said.

"Right do it your way," Martin shouted suddenly,

"but how can I find the bloody leak if the pump is stopped?"

"You will find it no problem," I answered,

"because its not a leak, it's a full blow of water." I turned away and walked over and had a word with the foreman saying,

"I need the pump shut off and the water in the Dam level with the Dock, then the pump started again and almost immediately shut off with no more than a differential of one to two feet below the level of the Dock."

Martin left the surface after I had the pump started and stopped instantly. Within minutes Martin screamed over the phone,

"Turn the pump off George, TURN IT OFF."

"Bobby turned it off before you went down" George said in an aggressive voice. Martin came back up straight away with two very sore knees, which had been sucked into the blow and barked up against the quay wall.

The following day Martin said nothing about carrying on with the job he had started and I found that, like Sandy McGill, he had never learned to weld or burn underwater either.
Nuttall's foreman had two sizeable plates cut for me out of 1 inch flat steel and I welded them over the two large blow holes. Martin was away from the boat for about two hours while I was working and Andrew told me it was because the sun was shining and he was sunbathing.

After we arrived back at our own berth that night and Martin had headed away to the hut Andrew said,
"You know Bobby, arrogance is bad enough but when it is coupled with ignorance it makes a hellish combination. You probably saved his life yesterday, but does he see it that way, no, in fact the way he was talking when you first went down, he was actually blaming you for his sore knees. At the same time, when does a standby diver go away sunbathing when his mate is underwater."

Chapter 8

The Dead Man's Brake

It was hot that afternoon, the Docks sweltered under the sun and the cobbled roadways shimmered as they reflected the heat from their curved hard surfaces. It was also very noisy. The rattle of the pistons of steam cranes hauling cargo out of ships' holds, and the squeal of wagon wheels protesting their lack of adequate lubrication as freight trains belched black smoke and hauled them slowly along the rails all mingled with the rumble of tons of coal sliding down the coal pans as steam driven ships filled their bunkers.

Henry Robb's steam lorries blew their whistles to warn everyone they were not constrained to following rails, as the Trains were. Tug boats sounded their shrill hooters and ocean going ships on the move answered with their bass baritone steam horns, all of which added to the cacophony of sounds which made up the orchestration of the Port's music.

The Tugs had also sounded their whistles to alert the dock deputy that they required the swing bridge to be swung open to allow them to take a merchant ship through the Albert to Edinburgh dock passageway. The dock deputy duly sounded his own warning siren and the bridge began to cantilever up out of its west end housing and slowly swung open. On the West side that the bridge had just left, and still a fair distance away was a freight train pulling ten wagons towards the open passageway.

  A shunts man trotted along in front of the train, a bright red cap on his head declared his job and a whistle hung on a short chain from his waistcoat, which he could use to warn unwary pedestrians of the Train's approach.

  He carried a long stout hook pole in one hand, with which he could hook or unhook the chains which linked all the wagons together, whichever was required. He moved to one side of the gap left by the open bridge and sat down on a mooring bollard. He glanced briefly at his oncoming train, still a good distance behind him, then turned his attention to the tugs manoeuvering the ship, as they lined her up and pulled her smoothly and skilfully through the passageway and into the Edinburgh Dock.

  Unconcernedly he drew a packet of cigarettes from his pocket and settled himself to have a smoke. He was, as always, glad of any respite from his continual trotting in front of his train. He watched the dock deputy in the glass house on the other side of the passageway pull on the levers and the bridge once more began lifting up its cantilever end clear of the chocks which had supported it opposite the shunts man, in preparation of swinging back across the gap again. Only now did the shunts man turn his head and look back at his oncoming steam Engine, to find it was almost abreast of him and he jumped up in sudden alarm and blew his whistle sharply to alert his driver to the danger.

The driver appeared to be slumped forward at the controls and the shunts man was powerless to do anything as the train rolled over and dropped down into the bridge recess and toppling sideways it carried on over the quayside and into the water of the passageway amidst a roar of an explosion of fire, steam and smoke. One by one five wagons were dragged over the side of the quay following the train and emptying their contents noisily into the passageway before the sixth one jack knifed with a screech and jammed on the top of the others and halted the remaining four as the horrified and speechless shunts man watched.

Martin was diving that day and on arrival at the scene Andrew immediately suggested it might be too dangerous to make the dive because of the precarious position the sixth wagon had finished up in. Martin stared hard at Andrew, then turned to George and said in a contemptuous manner.
"Just put the gear on me George."
"You will not be able to do anything anyway," Andrew argued,
"until a heavy duty crane arrives to lift away that dangerous wagon on top of the rest." Again Martin stared fixedly at Andrew before saying to him,
"Just you get me dressed and let me worry about cranes and danger." Andrew flushed up a high colour and said no more.
   I could not believe that Martin would make the dive before our Engineers and riggers made the wagons safe on top for him but that was exactly what he did and returned to the surface with the dead body of the train driver, which was passed up to the waiting Ambulance men. Martin then

remained standing on the diving ladder after his helmet was removed. The Engineer Foreman appeared above us and called down to him.

"Martin move your barge away until we clear the wagons up here, any one of them could topple sideways when we disturb them."

"What do you want me to move away for, you will need me to unshackle the underwater ones for you." Martin said stubbornly.

"We will clear the top five then give you a shout to bring your barge back into the passageway."

Martin's jaw jutted out in a manner I was beginning to recognise only too well as he glared up at the Foreman.

"Just you carry on with your own job and leave me to look after my end of the operation, my barge stays here" he said, and he then placed both elbows on top of the ladder's stringers and turned his head away and lowered it onto his forearms as if instantly asleep. The Foreman Engineer stood looking down at Martin's back for a few seconds, then shook his head and walked away out of sight.

Quite some time went by with Martin apparently unconcerned with anything that might be happening behind and above him, he did not even turn his head and look up at the vertical pile up of wagons fairly close to the barge. The crane arrived but the Foreman Engineer refused to attempt to remove the jammed wagon with our barge so close. I knew he was right and I could not understand why Martin seemed to deliberately court danger, when there was no need to do so whatsoever.

He would not even condescend to step up into the barge, instead he stood on the ladder with his boots still in the water and had actually stopped George from removing his front and back weights. For the life of me I could not understand this man's reasoning or mentality, he had no helmet on, which was the most dangerous thing of all.

The assistant Port Engineer, old Mr. Reid appeared in sight above us and called across to our barge,
"Martin, move your barge away out of the passageway altogether," Martin looked up instantly.
"Right Mr Reid we will shift away right round the corner now" he agreed. Andrew whispered ,
"Right Mr Reid we will shift away right round the corner now" in a quiet mocking tone. We pulled away into the Albert Dock and left them to it.

Some time after the whole job was completed and the train and it's wagons were lifted out of the passageway, we were told that a post mortem examination had proved the Locomotive driver had died of a sudden heart attack before he reached the passageway and although his train was fitted with a dead man's brake, which should stop it, if the driver's foot came off the pedal. This did not happen because the driver's foot remained on the dead man's brake after he collapsed and died.

Chapter 9

M.V. East Shore

Our linesman George Smiles was the only man in the team who was ages with myself. He and I struck up an immediate friendship, which sprang originally from our great love of fly fishing for trout and sea angling from a boat. Andrew Imrie, our second linesman, was considerably older than we were and had served in the second world war, as a sergeant in the army. Martin was the old man in the team and Jimmy Robertson our boatman lay somewhere in between.

One day we were lying in the lea of the east breakwater while the tide was at its lowest ebb. It was lunchtime and after eating the hot meal Jimmy had prepared for us, George said,
"Fancy climbing up on the breakwater and gathering a bucket full of mussels to use for bait on Saturday?"
We had planned to go on a sea angling trip that week on our own boat, which we kept moored in Dunbar harbour.
"Yes George, good idea, let's do that."

There was an easiness and friendliness that I shared with the whole team that would be foreign to Martin. His attitude towards his men bore a resemblance to the old Upstairs

Downstairs syndrome, where he kept them all at arms length, as if they were servants of his, and had to know, and keep their own place.

His high handed manner with them was partly responsible for the hatred they felt towards him. There was always a free and easy atmosphere in the boat as soon as he left it and today was no exception, for he had gone ashore to sunbathe on top of the east pier.

Before George and I climbed onto the breakwater Andrew asked,
"You haven't seen him sunbathing yet Bobby have you?"
"No Andrew I have not, why?"
"He lies spread eagled and stark naked with bits of matchsticks holding his fingers and toes wide apart to get the inside of them tanned. A man in his fifties carrying on like that, it's disgusting, it almost makes me sick." He was still shuddering at the thought, when we left him and climbed carefully on the slimy green stones of the harbour side of the east breakwater.

George and I walked over the crest of the breakwater to the seaward side and we both stopped dead, in front of us, on every side for as far as our eyes could see were hundreds of dead seagulls. There were small black headed gulls, Lesser Black Backs, Kittywakes and Herring gulls all strewn about the stonework of the breakwater.
"God" George said,
"what do you make of that Bobby?"
"Beats me George," I replied,
"but you can rest assured it is not the work of mink or any other predators, there are far too many of them." We had to pick our footfalls carefully around the dead birds as we

walked forward. Most of them lay with fully outstretched wings and with beaks gaping open, as if they had been fighting for breath, before they died.

I was studying them closely and came to the conclusion that they had not been dead for very long. There was no sign of putrefaction anywhere, or the inevitable presence of maggots, although they were swarming with sand flies. I was staring at a large herring gull lying on its right side with legs and wings sprawling and intertwined limply. Its left eye was wide open and looking up at me. Its beak gaped open exactly the same as all of the others around it.

Suddenly it slowly winked at me, and gave me a bit of a fright, somehow it seemed to be a knowing wink. I watched it closely for a few minutes and was just beginning to think I must have imagined it, when it slowly winked again. This bird was still alive but only just. We humans have eye lids that constantly blink to lubricate and clean our eyes. A bird has a nictitating membrane, which lies under its eyelid and has the same function as a windscreen wiper, only it is normally so fast it can hardly be spotted by a human eye, like the shutter of a camera.

This bird was so far gone that the membrane operated in slow motion. I gathered him up, very carefully supporting his neck and head, which lolled limply in all directions.

Back on the boat, I lined a large cardboard box with a spare set of my woollens and laid him inside, supporting his head and neck by building up the jerseys under them. The survey launch Figgate was alongside our diving boat and its crewman Arthur Robertson was sitting outside her cabin watching me.

"He is feenished Bobby," he called across, in a broad Shetland accent,
"you might as well jist thraw his neck noo and be done wi' it."

"Well we will see Arthur, I am going to give him every chance of recovery that I can."

The cabin of the diving boat was so warm that the butter in my locker was fairly soft, I scooped up a teaspoonful and placed it just inside the tip of the bird's open beak and no more. I arranged his head so there was only a slight downward incline towards his throat and left him alone after that.

We then set off, out into the Forth, to meet up with an oil rig supply ship that required our assistance. She was called the East Shore and earlier that day she had run down a trawler's net and picked up the trawl wire and wound it so severely around her propeller that it had crushed her rope guard on to her drive shaft and stopped her engine dead.

We soon came up on her, lying at anchor on the Granton side of the fairway. I climbed aboard to make sure the Chief Engineer had his engine in hand gear before I made the dive, even although I had been told the engine stalled, I still insisted it be put in hand gear, before I would go near her propeller. Satisfied, I dressed and tried to go under her stern, no way could I get near her prop for fish. The whole cod end was bulging with the trawler's catch and it had been wound up tightly under her stern. I had to destroy the net first by cutting it away with my knife. The lads sent me down some sacks, so we managed to get a fair share of the fish, before I sent the bulk of the catch to the bottom.

After clearing the net away and examining the damage I said,
"Take up my lines George, I'm coming up."
"Coming up it is, Bobby."
I stood on the diving ladder, after my helmet was removed and found myself looking at one of the saddest looking men I ever clapped eyes on. He was leaning over the side of the East Shore and he looked as if everybody belonging to him was dead.
"Why are you so sad?" I asked him,
"your ship has to be dry docked to have repairs done, so you should be looking forward to the best part of a week in port."
"This is not my ship," he said gloomily,
"that was my trawl net you just destroyed and it was my trawler that was run down by this ship."
"All the more reason for you to celebrate," I said,
"this is an American ship and she ran you down and destroyed your trawl net, that makes her liable for the lot."
His face lifted noticeably,
"Do you think so?"
"I know so, the yanks will fit you out with brand new gear, just so they can cover up the mistake they made, for their watch must have been asleep or drunk or something to run down a trawler in broad daylight in fine weather." He came along the deck to be nearer to me and whispered confidentially.
"All my gear was pretty old and well worn, do you think I could claim them for all new gear?"
"Listen, your gear was fine, your cod end was stretched tighter than the skin of a drum by the way it had been

wound up under the stern of this ship and yet it still held the whole of your catch until I hacked my way through your net to release it. I will be your witness if there is any argument about it, but I don't think the yanks will argue."
"Gee thanks diver," said the trawler owner as the gloomy look vanished from his face.

The East Shore's Captain would have none of it, when I said he would have to dry dock his ship to have the crushed rope guard removed and a new one fitted.
He asked me if I could cut away the damaged rope guard with the ship lying at anchor where she was and I agreed I could remove it with burning gear but I said that would mean he would be sailing without a rope guard from then on. This did not appear to worry him in the slightest, so off he went and sent his chief engineer along to have a word with me. The only concern the chief had was, could I be sure not to damage his drive shaft whilst burning away the guard. I assured him I would be cutting immediately behind its mounting, which would be well clear of the shaft itself and this I did, so the ship sailed into Leith and out again back to the oil Rigs minus a rope guard.

As we returned to our own berth, I looked at the herring gull, there was no change in his limp and lifeless looking condition. I gently lifted him out of his box and rearranged all the woollens before laying him back in again and shifting his body position from the one he had lain in all day and as I did so I noticed inside his gaping beak that there was only a fine trace of watery looking butter, which had plainly dribbled down the bird's throat. I placed a second small knob of soft butter just inside his mouth and satisfied I had made him as comfortable as I possibly could, we locked him in the cabin for the night, and as I left for home, I had grave doubts that I would find him still alive in the morning.

Chapter 10

Jonathan

The following morning I was up bright and early and set off for Leith Docks to see if the herring gull had survived the night or not. I had told Mabel and the girls about him the night before and they had promptly named him Jonathan Livingstone Seagull, after an article in the Readers Digest describing a book of the same name. I had also missed the BBC News bulletin warning the general public not to go near the dead gulls, which lay on the foreshore all over Britain. The newscaster said they had succumbed to some form of disease, which was contagious to humans.

After unlocking the cabin door of the diving boat and entering, I found there was no change in the bird's condition. I lifted him out of the box to find no mess underneath him, so setting him down carefully I rearranged all the woollens and placed him back inside the box in a different position to the one he had lain in all night. Yesterday's little knob of butter had gone, leaving only the greasy traces of its passage down the birds throat. He handled just like a rag doll, no movement from his body or head at all, after being laid in any position. My biggest worry was that I might inadvertently cause fluid to enter his lungs and choke him.

Nevertheless, I had to take a chance, for the signs of dehydration were only too obvious all around his inert body. I then gave him another tiny piece of butter to hold in the front of his mouth and set the angle of his head to the absolute minimum which would lead backwards towards his throat. I then carried his box into the compressor room, and through the port light I saw George jumping on board. He appeared in the doorway,
"Grievsie wants to see you," he said, followed by
"is the bird alive?"
"Right George," I answered.
"yes he is still alive, but only just and no more. I have set him in the corner of the compressor room, where he will get the heat from the diving pump, I will head back up now to see what David wants."

Entering David's office I found him sitting there with his fountain pen of invisible ink gyrating above the papers on his desk as usual, he looked up saying "Ah! Ha"
"You wanted to see me David."
"Yes eh! Bobby, there's a tractor eh! a tractor gone missing in the eh! Edinburgh Dock, we want you to eh! want you to go find it."
"Ok David, where exactly is it?"
"It's in the EDINBURGH DOCK, I just told you," he shouted angrily.
"Fine David but the Edinburgh Dock is a fair old size, can you give me an idea where to start looking?" I asked.

"How the bloody hell would I know where you should eh! where you should start looking, go and ask eh! go and ask the bloody Dockers."
"Oh the Dockers lost it, that's fine David, I will go and see them."
I think David realised his mistake in not telling me the Dockers lost it in the first place, for his anger vanished instantly. He picked up his rogue pen, lowered his head and said quietly,
"Aye just ask eh! just ask the Dockers Bobby son." I left him still struggling to force that obstinate fountain pen down onto the papers beneath it and write something.

With the crew aboard, we locked into the Edinburgh Dock and made for a large merchant ship we could see loading up. We tied up behind her and I went ashore to have a word with the Dockers. Turning into the dockside sheds adjacent to the merchant ship, I gasped at the sight before me. Four absolutely massive Ford tractors were awaiting their turn to be slung on board the ship. Standing beside one of them and reaching up with one arm, there was no way I could touch the top of its tyre, they were by far the biggest tractors I had ever seen.

I walked over to speak to the checker, whose job it was to mark off each item leaving the shed. He advised me to go and see the on board checker, because he had marked off the missing tractor as having left the shed, so I headed back to the ship. While talking to the checker on board the ship, I felt he knew more than he was prepared to say about the missing tractor, so I said to him.

"Nobody is going to get into trouble for giving me an idea just where to begin my search of the bottom, and it would save me an awful lot of scrabbling about in the thick silt on the bottom of this dock."

"Well I can only confirm it did not come on board this ship," he replied stubbornly.

"Look there is only one way a tractor of that size could have been lost over the side and that is by it being slung badly by the Dockers, do I start searching from the cross berth or the other side of the forward hold." He shook his head saying,

"I really can't say, all I know is it never came on board this ship."

"I will pick one area at random and you need say nothing at all, except for a nod or a shake of the head. There is no way you can be accused of knowing what has happened to the damned thing, if that is all you do." I could see he was still swithering so I took the bull by the horns.

"So, I might just start from the forward bollard her bows are moored to." He hesitated, and for a moment I thought he was not going to play my game. Then he gave the faintest little shake of the head, I pressed home my advantage.

"Or then again I might just start from the cross berth and work towards her stern." It took some moments before he reluctantly gave a very slight nod.

"Well" I said,

"I am sorry you are unable to help me and since you have no idea where it is, I will have to try pot luck instead." I tossed a coin in the air and catching it I flipped it over and pretended to look at the result.

"That's it then," I said,

"from the cross berth it is."

I left a very relieved checker in my wake as I walked back to the boat and called down to them to shift position all the way back to the cross berth.

I dressed and Andrew dropped the shot alongside the quay wall about twenty feet away from us and bringing the end of the line back to the boat, he handed it down to George, who made it fast to the diving ladder. I took hold of it from George and slipped off backwards into the water.

"On the bottom George," I said as I sunk into the soft silt up to my knees.

"On the bottom it is," George answered as I fell forward onto all fours on the soft surface of the silt. Turning my boots side on in a Charlie Chaplin style, I kicked off following the line until I came to the shot weight lying close to the quay wall. I let go of the shot line and untied the search line coiled up on the shot weight and running it out behind me I made my way back along the quay wall until the search line came taught. Now keeping the tension on it I began my first semi-circle by leaving the wall and heading out into the dock.

On the boat the boys would now be watching my bubbles describing a near perfect half circle. If I hit something with the search line then the regular pattern would suddenly alter and if I had not felt it, then the lads on the boat would soon tell me I was going around an obstruction of some kind on the bottom. There was nothing on that first sweep but on my second I felt the search pass around something and was instantly informed of this from the boat. Coiling up the line I began travelling in towards the centre and there she was, sitting on all four huge wheels.

"Ok George I have the tractor and I will wait here until you can send a crane down to me with lifting slings."

"Right Bobby, I will try and get you a crane as quick as I can." I now started to feel my way around the chassis of the massive tractor, for it would have been all the same if my helmet had no glass lights in it at all as there was not one blink of vision. I was staring into the blackest of all black nights, and I could see only the occasional tiny blips of light that my old mate Sandy McGill had once told me were minute fractions of daylight being carried down into our helmets along with our air supply. I often wonder if this is true or not. The crane took so long to come down to me that I had plenty time to feel my way all around the vehicle and determine exactly how I would sling it. The fact it was sitting in an upright position was the greatest help of all. I had no real problem when the crane finally arrived and I attached the four slings and up and away she went.

The job complete I turned my attention back to my patient. I lifted him back out of his box and still there was no mess under him. I was given a bit of a surprise as I did so, when Martin handed me some of his clean woollens saying,

"Put these under him Bobby, they are nice and soft," so much for the so called uncaring Martin. I thanked him and relined the bird's box with them and as I propped him back up inside I looked at the large curved beak, its slightly open mouth giving me the impression of a sardonic smile and as I watched he gave me that slow knowing wink once more. I did notice the membrane was slightly, only slightly, faster than before. I changed his position several times that day and I also fed him tiny pieces of cheddar cheese and butter.

At home that evening, I began thinking about the size of the tractors I had seen being loaded on board the ship. They were being shipped to Texas in America and I thought it was no wonder Texans got the name of being boastful Americans, if they kept comparing such things as their tractors with ours, I then sat down and composed a little poetry on the same subject, which I called,

The Boastful American

Tae auld Edinburry, frae Aiberdeen,
Angus came doon by train
Tae meet a guid American freend
arriving there by plane

They baith shook hands in manly way,
then traivelt intae toon
Intendin' north frae the Waverly
tae catch the train at noon

But oh! Whit a braggart he,
wad laugh at things sae sma'
An' tellt Angus Americee
had a' things twice as braw

"Call this a bridge," he finally speired
as ower the Forth they sped
"We have them twice as long" he sneered
"and four times the spread"
Then Angus says, richt puzzled sair
Wi' anxious face forlorn
"Ah dinnae ken, it wisna there
When ah came doon this morn."   Bob Sinclair- 1972

Chapter 11

The Iguana Ranger

A full seven days after I picked Jonathan up off the east break water he was still alive but the only improvement in his condition was the slight speeding up of his nictitating membranes over his eyes. This morning, however, there was a change. I lifted him out of his box to find the woollens under him had been slightly soiled by a mustard coloured liquid, not unlike the inside of a newly born baby's nappy. This was the first time anything had passed through his emaciated body and though he still hung like a wet dish cloth as I handled him, it was a sign that I was doing something right. In much better spirits I cleaned him up gently with lukewarm water and dried him off thoroughly, before placing him snugly back in his box wrapped in soft fresh woollens. I again adjusted his head to a slight backward angle and placed a very small piece of bread, soaked in warm water, into his mouth.

George was on the tiller and we had been locked in to the Imperial Dock by the Harbour Master. We sailed past the dry dock and I noticed it had a ship docking inside and they were preparing to pump the dock dry. I knew that by that night I would have some fresh sprats and small herring to add to, and augment my bird's meagre food intake.

We sailed on a little further up the east quay side and tied up alongside the ship, the Iguana Ranger, I went aboard to see her Chief Engineer. He had called for divers to make an examination of her Port side Propeller, which had begun juddering violently and caused him to shut down the port side engine. She was one of the larger of the oil rig supply ships, a twin screwed vessel, almost twice the size of the East Shore.

The Chief was a tall, muscular black man and he spoke with a delightful Jamaican accent. He already had both engines in hand gear, ready for us to make the dive under her. I returned to the diving boat and dressed and went below on a belly line slung under her stern. I found she had the usual four blades to each propeller and setting my boots to the level of the dead centre of the port prop's boss, I found each blade was taller than myself. The last six inches of all four blades had been bent back violently at an angle of almost 45 degrees towards her stern. I returned to the boat, stripped off and went back aboard to give the Chief the bad news.

I found him in the Captain's cabin. The Captain was a burly built South American man with a swarthy skin half hidden behind a beard of jet black hair. I explained to them both what I had found, then said,

"I am afraid you will have to dry dock to have a new propeller fitted." The Captain shook his head negatively.

"Can you not cut off the damaged ends of each blade?" he asked.

"Yes" I answered,
"I could do that but I would not be allowed to sign your clearance certificate for Insurance purposes."
"I don't need you to sign anything" the Captain said.
"We are registered in Panama and not with Lloyds of London, we have an eighteen month contract with only two months still to go, I can't afford to dry dock at this time, all I need is you to cut off the bent ends of the blades."
"Right Captain," I said,
"I can certainly do that for you."
"How do you go about doing that?" the Chief asked.
"Well, I first of all scribe each blade below the line of the damage to the worst one, to make all four blades equal in size and distance from the centre of the boss, to keep your bearings smooth, then I burn them off with an oxy-arc torch. There is just one thing Chief and that is I need to have each blade standing vertical to burn it, so your engineers will have to hand crank each blade into position for me before I can cut it."
"I will attend to that personally," the Chief said to my relief for he was obviously a very intelligent man.

 I returned to the boat and we settled down to await the arrival of a lorry with our burning gear and Generator. I explained to the lads we would get a good drink when we finished at 5 pm and it would all be paid for by the scrap value of the cut off bent pieces from the propeller.

 When the lorry arrived the lads began readying the gear, while I went back on board the ship to tell them I was ready to start. I was taken aback when the Captain told me the job was cancelled. He sat with his shoulders slumped forward in a crestfallen state.

"Your Boss, Mr Grieve phoned me and told me it is not possible to cut phosphor bronze under the water."
"I see" I said,
"just like the bumble bee eh!?"
"Come again?" the Captain said, so I told him the story about the aeronautical experts who had all agreed that the bumble bee's wings were far too small, and its body was far too big and heavy, so no matter how fast its wings could beat, it was physically impossible for the bumble bee to fly but no one thought to tell this to the bee, so it just carried on flying regardless.
"What's your point?" the Captain asked.
"Captain, nobody ever told me it's impossible to cut phosphor bronze under the water, so I have been doing it for more years than I care to remember."
The Captain sat upright and his face cleared instantly.
"You mean you can do it?" he said hopefully.
"Of course I can" I answered.

Back on the diving boat, I dressed and went under the Iguana Ranger once again. I now had a small staging slung from her stern to stand on, and I soon had all four blades scribed to guide my cutting. I called up to the boat to send me down a light line with a shackle on it. It duly arrived and I blew a small hole through the bent top of the first blade and fitted the shackle through the hole. Now I could cut with confidence and the bent part would drop off and be pulled up to the boat once it swung clear.

The length of the scribe, or in other words the cut was about 2 feet 9 inches long, so quite sizeable pieces would be sent up to the boat. The Chief cranked up each blade for me in turn, as I cut them and soon we were finished, job complete.

Standing on the diving ladder, before my helmet was removed. I could see all was not well on the boat. The glum faces of George and Andrew spelt out some form of disaster. As soon as George lifted the helmet clear, I said
"Tell me about it, what has happened?"
"The Captain just left us before you came up." said Andrew and George added,
"He took away the phosphor bronze cuttings, saying he had to produce them as evidence to show his Bosses." This meant no dram and pint for the team that night, paid for by the scrap value of the phosphor bronze cuttings.

We did stop off at the dry dock, on our way back and picked up a pockle of small sprats and herring caught against the sieves of the dry dock pumps, as they emptied the dock.

At half past 4 that evening we were in the diving hut, I was filling in the diving diary and Martin was reading his newspaper. Martin laid down his paper and said very quietly "Any chance of teaching me how to use the burning gear, Bobby." I was taken aback by Martin's request but answered immediately.
"Of course Martin, no problem, I will have you burning with it in jildi time." It brought back a memory of the time I had said exactly the same thing to big Sandy McGill before the start of the Cockenzie job almost ten years ago.

In the privacy of the diving hut I gave Martin a crash course on the use of oxy-arc burning gear.

The following morning I was again the first man aboard the diving boat, to look after my invalid bird and I felt a mixture of emotions as I looked at Jonathan. His head was upright, clear of the supporting woollens and his beak was closed. His eye turned up to look at me and his thrapple moved slowly up and down visibly inside his throat, but my elation was tempered by the sight of his nakedness. He looked like a plucked chicken, all his wing and body feathers had fallen out and lay there on either side of him inside the box, only his tail feathers were still attached to his body. His head remained upright as I lifted him out of his box and laid him down gently on the bench seating.

He watched me as I cleaned out the mess in the bottom of his box and spread newspapers around inside before placing fresh woollens in after them. I lifted him back inside the box and as soon as I opened my locker and took out the plate filled with small sprats, he turned his head upwards and his beak opened wide. I popped a sprat inside and watched his gullet slowly distend and move up and down in slow motion and the sprat was gone. I fed him another two, for they were very small fish and I gave him his usual small knob of butter just inside his mouth as lubrication. All in all I felt there was a marked improvement in the bird's overall condition, if I discounted the sudden moult.

Chapter 12

Of Rope and Smithereens

The following day I was again surprised when I unlocked the door of the diving boat's cabin, for Jonathan was standing bow legged on the bench seating clear of his box. I could not stop myself from laughing at the ludicrous sight he presented as I entered the cabin. He turned his head on one side and looked up at me, out of an eye which now shone with crystal clear clarity and was completely at odds with the nakedness of his whole body. The scrawny neck only added to the plucked chicken look he presented, but now the bare quills of his tail feathers, which had survived the moult, stuck out from his bottom as if some miniature bow man had discharged a quiver of tiny arrows into his bum. The vestiges of feathers still remaining on their upper ends completed the suggestion of the flights of small arrows.

The bench he stood on was dotted all over with small pure white splotches of his droppings. Andrew jumped aboard followed by Martin, Andrew hung in the doorway and exclaimed.
"Oh! For God's sake, what a bloody mess, are we supposed to clean that lot up every day?"

"No" I answered him,

"I will clean it up and I will be aboard earlier in the mornings to do it from now on, since the bird is on the mend," to my surprise Martin said,

"I will come in early and give you a hand with him Bobby." This was the second indication I had, that showed Martin's concern for helpless creatures and gave the lie to Andrew's alleged Germanic arrogance and selfishness, that he attributed to Martin.

The steam tug Oxcar arrived to escort our diving boat out to the Western harbour, close to Rank's flour mill, where the day before I had examined a boulder to be destroyed using underwater explosives. The boulder had been left high above the seabed in the wake of the dredger, which had excavated the bottom all around it. As we cleared the end of the West pier, we could see and hear the Goliath dredger tearing the bottom out close to Henry Robb's shipyard. The boulder we were heading towards was a saddle shaped volcanic rock about eleven feet long six wide and seven feet high and it lay directly in the path of what was intended to be the fairway for deep sea Liners, which one day would moor up alongside the wharf in front of the flour mill.

In the cabin of the diving boat I prepared two pannier bags containing a total of three pounds each of pentonite primaries and submarine gelatine dynamite. I fully expected this charge to be only one of at least two or three I would have to use on such a hard igneous rock before destroying it completely. I dared not increase the charges, for now we were only about three hundred yards away from the flour mill. Martin dressed and took down the charge and after he returned on board, I had the tug pull us back and requested

permission from the harbour Master to fire. This granted, I set her off and Martin prepared to dive again and have a look at the result. In the meantime I began collecting the dead fish which were floating up from the bottom, by scooping them on board with a long handled pock net. This was both for ourselves and the smaller herring and sprats for Jonathan. After I finished collecting the fish, I moved closer to the diver phone to await Martin's report. We watched his bubbles going around in a large circle, stopping still for a few minutes, then returning in the opposite direction. I looked at George and Andrew.
"I don't think he is going to tell us," I said.
"He will be trying to get his brain in gear," Andrew said.
"There is something bothering him," George said.
"that's what he always does when something baffles him, he goes completely silent." I depressed the speak switch,
"Any luck, Huck?" I asked.
"You are not going to believe this" Martin said,
"you have blown it to bits." I shook my head at the lads,
"No way has six pounds of jelly blown that baby to bits," I said, then depressed the switch again and spoke to Martin.
"What size are the bits Martin?"
"There are no bits, you have blown the hell out of it" he answered.
"Martin there must be bits of some size around you down there, there must be?"
"There is absolutely nothing, you have blown it to SMITHEREENS" Martin said in an excited voice
"Can you describe to me what the bottom looks like where it was originally?" I asked.

"It's just sand" he said, "all sand, with a big crater in the bottom." I smiled at the lads, for now I understood what had happened.

"Can you go down in the crater and see what is in the bottom of it?"

"Right, going down now" he said, and a few minutes later he exclaimed,

"Aw! Wait a minute, the top of the boulder is just showing in the very bottom of the hole and it just has a few cracks across it."

"Can you lie down in the bottom, if it is possible Martin, so I can read your depth?" I asked.

"Right Bobby I can do that alright, lying flat now" he said, I looked at his depth gauge,

"Ok Martin, you are reading 44 feet deep, so that boulder must have been resting on a soft want in the bottom and the charge punched it straight downwards out of the way altogether. You can come up, because it is now below the level that the dredger is working to, so that's us finished."

On the way back to our berth, I brought a plate of small sprats into the cabin and Jonathan promptly jumped out of his box and waddled wide legged towards me across the bench seating. This was unusual for a herring gull, because normally they walk as straight forward as we humans do, so I guess his Penguin like waddle was a sign of the weakness that still existed in his legs. The little look alike arrows in his bottom swayed comically from side to side as he approached me. He knew what he wanted and reaching me, he cocked his head on one side and stared up at me one eyed for a few moments then slowly opened up his beak as wide as he could and showing him I understood his message, I popped in some very small sprats which he swallowed slowly. He then waddled back to his box and climbed back inside it and slumped down, obviously exhausted, but I was happy, for my boy was certainly on the mend.

Although George was on the tiller as we returned towards our berth, he jumped down into the cockpit for a minute to pass a message from the tug skipper.
"Grievsie wants us to go alongside a ship lying just outside the Victoria Dock gates, he has had our barge towed over there with our burning gear aboard. Her Captain says his propeller has been fouled by a very heavy wire and we are to go straight there and burn it off, because he is waiting to sail to London." I looked at Martin and gave him a secret wink.
"Well you are diving today Martin," I said
"so you better get dressed again." Andrew gave me a hard look, but said nothing, as Martin sat back down on the dressing stool.

When we arrived at the ship, we gave the tug a wave of goodbye and moored alongside our own diving barge. The ship was one of the bulk cement carriers that operated between Leith and London and belonged to the actor Brian Rix. I climbed on board and had the Chief Engineer put his engine in hand gear to protect my buddy. It would be a disaster if an engineer made a mistake and engaged the propeller while a standard suit diver was alongside of it.
By the time I climbed back on board the diving barge, Martin was already down below the ship's stern, I moved to

the diver phone. Martin was grunting with some sort of struggle he was having with something or other.

"How is it Martin?" I asked.

"is there a lot of wire around her prop?"

"No, there are only about six turns but it is a very heavy wire, I would say about 2 inch diameter and I had to fight my way in past the first two coils which have figure eightied into a solid ball."

"That's nasty stuff Martin, watch out for whiplash when you cut it."

"Aye but I am too old and too fly for that Bobby." Martin answered with a laugh. Andrew muttered,

"Aye you are fly right enough you bent nosed bugger." George turned and asked me,

"What's the idea of letting him do this, he has never burned anything before?"

"George" I said,

"he shocked the hell out of me last night when he asked me if he could have a go sometime at the oxy-arc burning and would I show him how the gear works"

"Show him how it works" Andrew remarked dryly,

"I will not be surprised if he blows a hole right through his own helmet, you are taking a chance Bobby, he is as thick as two planks of wood."

"Knife switch on" Martin called.

"Knife switch on" I repeated and nodded at big Arthur, who had been sent over by David Grieve as a spare hand to work with us on this job. The big man threw over the switch and I reported back to Martin.

"The knife switch is on, Martin." Several minutes went by and I realised it was not happening,

"Martin can I turn the knife switch off for a moment?" I asked.

"Yes whatever" he replied in a weary voice. I had Arthur switch off then said.

"The knife switch is off, Martin, can I ask you where you clamped the earth lead about?"

"I stuck it on the end of the rope guard" he answered.

"Maybe it would be better clamped on one of the blades of the propeller," I suggested.

"Ok I will change it over now."

"See" Andrew said gloatingly,

"even I know the rope guard is clear of the shaft. I told you he would make an arse of it." I ignored his caustic remarks.

"Ok that's it fast to the blade of the propeller, so you can put the switch back on again." Martin said

Arthur threw it back on and I said.

"Knife switch is on Martin," almost immediately we could hear the thrum of the arc and see the flashes of bright light under the ship's stern, within seconds we could also see the acrid fumes rising from the surface of the water. He was burning away fine. Alas it only continued for a few minutes, then all was silent once again. I was now worried because Martin had not called for the knife switch to be turned off.

"There is something bothering him again," George said, he seemed to know his diver's moods better than anybody else.

"I bet I know what he has done," said Andrew.

"he has probably blown a hole in the propeller shaft, I wouldn't put it past him."

Now that did alarm me and I instantly called to Arthur to cut the power to the torch without an order from Martin.

"What's happening Martin?" I asked.

"It was going fine but the bloody thing won't burn the centre part of the wire," he shouted in exasperation.
"I have been stabbing at it for ages but it will not burn."
"Martin" I said quietly,
"I have turned the knife switch off at the moment."
"What the hell did you do that for?" he said angrily.
"No wonder I can't burn the centre bit of the wire."
"Martin, the centre core of every heavy wire is rope, and you can't strike an arc in rope, so take out your knife and cut through it and it will drop away."
There was a long pause, which gave Andrew time enough to say.
"I told you Bobby the man is brainless, I would not trust him with a kiddie's toy boat, never mind a real ship."
"Sorry Bobby" Martin said contritely,
"I completely forgot the centre of every heavy wire is a rope core, I feel so stupid."
"First time I ever heard him admit he was wrong about anything at all, you are being honoured Bobby," George said.
" Yes" Andrew agreed,
"he normally has no idea how stupid he is, the ignorant big German bastard." by God how Andrew Imrie hated Martin, It was frightening to think too deeply about that. A man who held his diver's life in his hands every time that diver slipped below the surface of the sea but Martin finished the job successfully and signed the ship as fit to sail, and off she went to London.

We returned to our own berth, this always seemed to please Jonathan, for as soon as the diving compressor stopped and quietude returned to the cabin, he would climb out of his box and waddle fearlessly among us. He never failed to make his intention clear, by stopping and staring up at any one of us, with an imperious lift of his head, followed by the wide gape of his bill, which spoke volumes to us all.

We would often be sitting enjoying our afternoon coffee and biscuits and we would be joined by our featherless friend who, it seemed determined, if we were feeding, then he had a right to feed as well. Even the supposed hard hearted Andrew would laugh at his antics as the bird alternated between furiously paddling with both webbed feet and then offering his gaping jaws to each one of us in turn until Andrew asked if he could feed him some sprats. So Jonathan slowly worked his magic over the whole diving team and had us all, metaphorically speaking, eating out of the palm of his hand, in no time at all.

Chapter 13

Jonathan Decorator

Over the next three weeks Martin was as good as his word and arrived early every morning to help me clean up the diving boat cabin. This was just as well, for Jonathan had lost his appetite and found a horse's. Originally the inside of the cabin was painted Battle ship grey but it appeared as if the bird disagreed with the décor and did his best to re-decorate it, in brilliant white. How he managed to get so far up the bulkheads and the boat's sides, without wing feathers to lift him was a bit of a mystery but it was also a testimony to his resourcefulness and returning strength

His legs were now as straight as a die and he could jump from one side of the bench seating to the other with no trouble at all. When he did leap across the full width of the boat, some form of reflex action caused him to beat his featherless wings in a futile attempt to fly across.
The little arrows of his bottom feathers remained unchanged but the rest of his body and wings had an all over stubble of tiny freshly growing feathers peeping through his skin.

One morning Martin and I were standing outside David Grieve's office after cleaning up the boat. The 8 am whistle blew and Martin knocked on David's door.

"Come in" came a voice from within and we both entered. David sat head down and as usual his right hand was describing small circles above the papers on his desk, as if once more he was determined to force his recalcitrant fountain pen to descend and write something. He gave up and laid the pen down, looked up at us and said, "Ah! Ha!"

"Timber wharf's Victoria Dock, with the carpenters today David" said Martin, in a mild mannered tone of voice.

"Oh! No you are NOT" David said in a loud irritable tone, quick as a flash Martin said loudly,

"Oh! so is it hate the divers week again Dave eh!" David gave an ingratiating smile as he replied,

"No no Martin, nothing to do with eh! to do with hate the divers week, ha ha ha, you have to, hee hee, to eh! to see the harbour Master. There's a ship in eh! a ship in some sort of eh! some sort of trouble so go and see eh! go and see the Harbour Master."

"Right David" Martin replied in a normal tone of voice.

"We will go and see the Harbour Master now."

David picked up his pen and once more looked down at the papers on his desk. It was obvious we were dismissed so he could concentrate on his never ending struggle with the obstinate fountain pen.

I met the Harbour Master, Douglas Gray for the first time and was immediately impressed by the character of this man. His sturdily built frame was of average height and a larger than usual head was topped by short, well groomed grey hair. His direct manner showed an easy confidence of being in charge and was softened somewhat by a lazy grin that would spread over his rather florid features whenever he spoke.

I would discover later, that during the war he served aboard the oil tanker the Ohio, as a young first officer. The ship was attacked by the Luftwaffe in the Mediterranean, whilst she was part of a convoy attempting to reach and assist the island of Malta. The convoy was decimated by the bombers and the Captain of the Ohio was killed. Douglas took over and brought her into Valletta harbour on the island with her decks awash and thereby saved her precious cargo of oil. She was one of only a few ships which survived the ariel bombardment.

He was then given command of an armed trawler to bring back home safely to the U.K. and decided to run the gauntlet in the dead of night. He sailed her successfully across the Mediterranean and through the straits of Gibralter then he thought his luck had run out in the Bay of Biscay. As the morning of the fourth day dawned, he was spotted by a Heinkel bomber which dived in to attack. Douglas started zig-zagging his small craft while his gunner fired at the enemy. A plume of smoke shot out backwards from the plane's tail and moments later it exploded and plunged into the sea. Douglas and the gunner were both decorated for their remarkable feat.

A quiet unassuming man, it was always a pleasure to be in his company from that first meeting onwards. The Deputy Harbour Masters were Captain Henderson and the youngest was Captain Alan Childs. All three were alike in one respect for they shared the same gentlemanly manner, no matter who they were dealing with.

The job turned out to be another oil rig supply ship with a heavy wire around her propeller. She had been towed into the port by the tug Craigleith and now lay moored in the Victoria Dock awaiting our arrival. We moored our barge alongside the ship and I went aboard to see the Chief Engineer as usual. I soon discovered she was an American ship and the cook told me I would find the chief in the Captain's cabin, I knocked on the door and a voice called, "Come in" in a broad Yankee accent. I walked in to get one of the real shocks of my life, there were four people present in the cabin. One man sat sprawling in an armchair smoking a small cigar, he wore a dressing gown bunched up around his shoulders and upper body but from the waist down he was completely naked. Sitting on a rug on the floor near to him was a beautiful auburn haired girl, a really stunning looking female, wearing absolutely nothing at all. She held a cigarette in her hand and turned her head to look unconcernedly at me as I entered.

In another armchair there sat a second man resting one arm on his knee, while his other leg was tucked up under his chair, he too was smoking, what looked like a large Havana cigar. He was also stark naked and his manhood dangled below the armchair seat in full view. Stretched out on her back on a couch was the fourth member of the group. She was an equally terrific looking natural red head, which her complete nakedness attested to.

"Port divers," I offered,
"I am looking for the Chief Engineer." They all showed not the least bit of concern regarding their appearance and their attitude seemed to suggest they might just as well have been respectably clad in evening dress and ball gowns.

"Oh! Yeah diver," said the large Havana smoker, sitting upright now.
"come to remove that blasted wire from our screw have you," he drawled.
"Yes Chief," I answered,
"but I need your engine in hand gear before I go below."
"Ok diver have a word with my second, in the engine room and he will fix you up." He leaned over and lifted a glass from a small table, close to his chair, he swallowed its amber coloured liquid in one gulp,
"tell him you have just had a word with me diver ok."
"Fine Chief" I replied as I withdrew and closed the cabin door behind me.

I returned to the barge, after seeing the Second Engineer engage the hand gear. George and Andrew dressed me and I dived below the ship's stern. There I found a veritable hawser was wound loosely around the rope guard and propeller and if that was not enough, there was also a sizeable amount of a heavy Manilla mooring rope mixed among the coils of the hawser. I straddled the rope guard behind the twisted turns of wire and rope and began burning the hawser with confidence, for the cut off pieces sprang sideways away from me as they fell to the dock floor. The wire was easy but not so the Manilla mooring rope. Even though my Siebe Gorman diving knife was as sharp as a razor, it still took some hacking to cut through it and here I forgot the old Royal Naval adage of

'Always cut away from your thumb, and towards your chum.' I was holding on to the rope with my left hand while I sawed and hacked my way through it with my right hand. I began to slice, using a chopping motion and as I did so the blade was deflected off one of the turns of the hawser and it came down in a slicing motion across the base of my left thumb.

The heavy duty rubber glove probably saved me from severing my thumb altogether, but nevertheless I had sliced it to the bone. I whipped off the glove and stared in dismay at the blood gushing out of the wound.

"George can you send me down a lint dressing and a bandage from the first aid box, I have just cut my thumb open."

"Ok Bob, I take it you are not coming on board."

"No George I am sitting on the rope guard so I will bandage it and carry on." When the bandage came down to me I applied it and used the last part of it to lash the thumb backwards to my left wrist as tight as I could, to close up the gaping cut. Although I felt no pain at that time, I knew the rest of the job would be pure agony, for one of the strange anomalies of oxy-arc burning is the way the electricity attacks any wound or break in human skin, whether a diver is wearing rubber gloves or not. Another strange result of electrolysis shows up when we have not been burning or welding for quite a while. Our helmets become tarnished with a green verdigris and all the brass work becomes faded and dull in colour. One burning or welding job later and the helmet gleams like new and you can see your reflection in the bright brass work. I have often wondered what the electrolysis might be doing to our heads inside the helmets.

With the thumb bandaged and tied back I carried on with the job, gritting my teeth at the stabbing pain while burning through the hawser and glad of the respite when cutting one handed through the mooring rope. After clearing it all away,

I examined the propeller and the rope guard, to be sure there was no damage that I would have to report to the ship's Chief Engineer. I then surfaced and stripped off my woollens and went aboard to report she was fit for sea.

In the main accommodation of these ships, the stairways are very narrow and so steep it feels like you are climbing up a near vertical ladder. I reached the foot of the stairway, which led up to the Captain's cabin and coming down from the top was the statuesque figure of the red headed girl. She was just as I had last seen her, naked as the day she was born, except for a pair of high heel shoes, which clip clopped as she came down the steep stairs. I stepped inside the cooks galley at the bottom of the stairs, to allow her to pass by, but on reaching me, she smiled sweetly and intimated she wished to enter the galley. Embarrassed I squeezed past her out thrusting breasts and stepped into the narrow alleyway and allowed her to enter.

"Captain says he would like a fresh pot of coffee and another bottle of brandy," the girl said to the burly Cook, who was busy preparing vegetables on his chopping board. The Cook glanced around at the glamorous naked girl saying,

"Ok honey, help yourself to a bottle of Napoleon and I will bring up the coffee shortly." The girl vanished into the Cook's storeroom and seeing my astonished look the Cook grinned at me, winked and said.

"Like a drink yourself diver?"

"I would like a coffee please," I answered,

"can't take anything else while I am diving." The girl reappeared carrying a bottle and clip clopping out of the galley, she began to ascend the steep stairway, her hips swaying from side to side and leaving a view of her rounded bottom that will forever be burned in my brain.

"Thank you Cookie" she called over her right shoulder, as she turned into the Captain's cabin.

"I feel as if I have stepped into a nudist colony on this ship." I said after the girl had gone.

"Ah! You Scots get all up tight with nakedness, whereas it's nothing to us Americans," said the Cook, handing me a mug of coffee.

"I suppose you are right there Cook but I never saw anyone less concerned with nakedness than these four up there" I said nodding my head upwards.

After finishing my coffee I climbed the stairs, knocked on the Captain's door and entered to give my report. All four had glasses of brandy in their hands and I politely refused the Captain's offer of a drink for myself.

"No problems then diver?" asked the Chief Engineer, lolling back in his chair.

"None at all Chief everything is in good order and completely undamaged."

"What have you done to your hand?" the Captain asked.

"Well I burned off the wire no bother, but there was also a Manilla mooring rope round the screw and while cutting it away with my knife I sliced through my own thumb." The brunette was still sitting on the carpet and she hugged her knees and exclaimed,

"Oh! That must have been painful," and her breasts jiggled as her shoulders shuddered at the thought. I signed the Captain's certificate and took my leave of their small nudist colony.

At 4 o'clock that afternoon we were back at our own berth and I discovered all the little look alike arrows of Jonathan's tail feathers were lying outside his box. I felt sure he had plucked them all out himself as I watched him rubbing his body and wing plumage gently with his beak. He appeared to be smoothing out the fibres of his new baby feathers as they were growing into place.

He had developed the habit of alternately tapping his feet on the bench seating the moment I entered the cabin. Both webbed feet would go up and down in a pit-pat, pit-pat, pit pat at real speed. This I knew was a ploy used by some birds to fool earth worms that heavy rain was falling and when successful, a worm would raise its head slightly above the earth and be promptly grabbed by the bird and forcefully dragged out of the ground. Jonathan used it to signify he was hungry, so I encouraged him, by feeding him every time he did it.

My father's firm of Young and Leslie Stevedores had their offices and gear shed in Tower Street just outside the Docks and close to the old Sailors Home for many years, but now the firm had changed it's name to Leslie and Saddler and they had taken over the No. 4 Outer Harbour shed beside our berth. This meant Dad was permanently based close by us and was able to come and see Jonathan on a regular basis. That night, just about 5 o'clock, I was waiting for him to come along from his shed, to give him a lift home in my car. I was standing at the caisson gate of the Prince of Wales dry Dock watching Dad come walking towards me.

The 5 o'clock whistle blew and I could see Willie Riddle, the pump house man of the adjacent Alexandra Dry Dock, leaving his pump house and heading towards his car, which he always left parked close to his dry dock gates. He climbed into his car, just as my old man was nearing me.

Willie started up the engine but instead of driving away like I had seen him do a hundred times, his car suddenly leapt backwards and vanished down into his own dry dock. The Dock was dry, with a ship in it and for a moment or two I hesitated, thinking, did I really see what I thought I saw, Dad came up to me and I asked him.

"Dad did you see that?"

"See what?" he asked and I immediately set off running across the caisson.

"Willie Riddle just reversed his car down into his own Dry Dock" I called back, as I raced across the Alex's own gates and saw the car lying in the bottom of the dock, with Willie hanging out of the driver's door. He was dead and turning a purplish blue when I reached him.

Oh! God, I thought, if only the dock had been full of water I might have saved him, for at that time I had the ability to dive in fully clothed and not only reach the bottom but stay there without breathing for more than three minutes. Alas it was not to be, for Willie had obviously died the instant his car hit the bottom of the dock.

Chapter 14

The Suicide

It was the month of March and the water of Leith river was in full spate, colouring all the water throughout the Docks a light brown with suspended silt. From our boat the opaque mixture did not allow us to see more than a few inches below the surface. The violent confluence of the fresh water meeting the salt of the sea continued all the way past the cellular dam and invaded the western harbour as well.

We were on our way out the fairway to search for a large anchor lost from our own Digger. The turmoil of the heavier gravity sea water clashing with the fresh, produced a similar effect to that of a partly opened sluice and a fair old boil was showing ahead of us, where the brown river water met the clear water of the sea.

Andrew suddenly pointed and said.
"What's that?" he raised his hand to shield his eyes and moments later he said.
"I could have sworn I saw a body on the surface up ahead of us about forty feet away."

I immediately cut our speed to slow ahead and we all scanned the swirling surface water in front of us. Up from the depths came the body of a young woman dressed in a floral print dress, she was no more than twenty feet ahead of our boat and as we watched, she was carried under once more by the turbulent current and I immediately stopped our engine. As we drifted onwards we watched on either side of our boat and Martin pulled on a pair of rubber gloves. George grabbed our boat hook and Andrew took hold of the long handled pock net. Minutes later she surfaced once more, close to our starboard side and George managed to pull her closer with the boat hook. The backwash and undertow threatened to draw her down again but Martin leaned over the side and grabbed hold of her arm.

The lads quickly removed our staging which was lashed down on top of the cabin and passed it under her. Using the two ropes bridled and shackled to the staging, on each corner, we heaved her on board and lifted her up on top of the roof of the cabin. She had obviously been in the water for some time and although the ice cold water had slowed down the process of decomposition, nevertheless the smell of decaying flesh was horrible.

We turned the boat around and made our way back towards the docks and informed the Harbour Master that we had a dead body on board. "Phew" said Jimmy,
"what a guff, I will be glad to see her off the boat as quickly as possible." Andrew stood on top of the cabin looking down at the corpse.
"I would say she was a woman in her early forties" he said. I glanced up at her from the cockpit, a pair of scruffy, white down at the heel shoes were still on her badly swollen feet. The Harbour Master instructed us to moor up to the

quayside outside the Imperial lock entrance to await the arrival of the C.I.D.

Two plain clothes police detectives duly arrived and an ambulance followed shortly after. They were in no hurry to take her off the diving boat and one man began to take photographs of the dead woman from many different angles. The other officer took statements from us regarding exactly where we were when we found her. After he had satisfied himself that he had written down all the relevant facts of her discovery he said,
"We have been looking for her for over two months."
"Oh!" I said, "so you knew her?"
"We knew her right enough, she was one of Leith's well known hoors (Old Scot's word for whores) and plied her trade in the Port for many years."
"I thought I knew her face," said Martin.
"Did you now," said the instantly animated Detective,
"and just exactly how well did you know her?"
"No, I mean, I mean, I feel as if I have seen her in the Docks from time to time," said Martin hurriedly, obviously terrified the policeman might get the wrong idea that he would have anything to do with prostitutes.
"How did you know she was missing?" I asked. The policeman's serious looking face relaxed,
"Some of her mates told us they were worried she was becoming suicidal. At first we were not unduly worried, for she would sometimes go off in a ship to the continent and be back in a fortnight or so. Then we got a report from one of her mates that she had said she was going to throw herself

off Bernard Street bridge into the water of Leith." He paused and lit a cigarette inhaling it strongly.

"God what a stench," he remarked before continuing

"As time went by, we did become concerned at her long absence and we broke into her house in Royal Park Terrace, there, we found she had left a suicide note confirming she was about to jump off Bernard Street Bridge. Her two favourite pubs were on either side of the Bridge, the 'Man at the Wheel' on the one side and the 'Kings Wark' on the other, so we had to consider she might have taken enough drink in a depressed state some night and decided to end it all and it now appears that's exactly what she did."

At last they removed her from the boat and the lads scrubbed down everything with disinfectant but it did not completely remove that lingering odour, which was still discernible for days after the event. We then set off back towards our own berth and since the Digger's lost anchor would have to wait until another day, the lads began to blow down the Diving pump's air reservoirs. This was always very noisy and something that Jonathan hated, for the high pressure air would hiss out violently and every so often it would form into an ice bullet, so dense it was capable of blocking the remaining high pressure air. It took about thirty seconds of silence before the ice warmed up and melted sufficiently for the bullet to be ejected with a loud bang and with such incredible force it smashed to bits against the metal guard plate under the discharge nozzle. Jonathan always vacated the compressor room as soon as the lads started blowing down.

Today he joined me on the stern of the boat and hopped up on to the transom. I had decided that I would allow him to return to the wild whenever he wanted to go but although he cocked his head on one side to stare up at the Herring gulls flying above our boat he had not, as yet, shown any inclination to fly off with them.

On the following Sunday I was at home and telling Mabel and my three youngest daughters about Jonathan. All three, Fiona, Rosslyn and Pamela started pleading to be allowed to see him and Mabel said,
"Could you not take us down to the Docks today and let the girls see him?" to the delight of all four I agreed to take them down and I also loaded the baby's bath into the car to take with us. When we arrived at the diving boat, I left the girls and Mabel in the car while I climbed on board to clean up the cabin. Jonathan watched me with what seemed like a disapproving look, as if I should not be concerning myself with needless things like cleaning up his mess. He marched back and forth across the bench seating in an attempt to bring my eyes to bear on the far more important signal of his wide open beak. I ignored him and brought the family on board.

They sat on my dry woollens laid out on the damp bench seating and stared at the bird opposite them. Jonathan stared back, fearlessly, then he had them all laughing as he began his little war dance of pit pat, pit pat, pit pat with both webbed feet until I gave in and opened my locker and fed him with some small sprats. I then placed the baby bath on the floor between the seats and began filling it with the fresh water hose. Jonathan watched this new spectacle with interest, head on one side and one eye cast down from the bench seat. He was an intelligent bird and as soon as I finished filling the bath, he jumped down into it and began shovelling water over his head and back and fluffing out his new feathers to wash them. He also began beating his wings in the water and ignored the squeals of laughter coming from the wee girls he was soaking.

This was a day I would never forget, seeing Mabel and my young daughters so happy watching the antics of the bird and knowing my boy Jonathan had now made an almost full recovery from his near death experience. At the same time I also felt a deep sadness for the young woman who had decided to end it all, by drowning herself in the freezing water of Leith river. We will never know what caused such desperation in her inner soul to make her choose such a horrible way out.

Chapter 15

The Leg

The 8 am whistle blew and Martin knocked on David Grieve's office door as usual. "Come in" came from inside and we entered together. David sat head down, scribbling furiously with his fountain pen, which again, I noticed was still resolutely refusing point blank to leave the slightest mark on the papers under it. David laid the pen aside, looked up at Martin and said "Ah! Ha!"
"We are examining Berths in the Imperial Dock today David" Martin said.
"Right Martin" David agreed,
"and at the same eh!, the same time you are to keep your eh! keep your eyes open for eh!, keep your eyes open for a leg."
"Right David we will keep our eyes open for a leg" said Martin as David once more dismissed us by taking up his pen and again studying the blank papers lying in front of him.
    We both withdrew and began walking over towards the diving boat and I said to Martin,
"What does keep your eyes open for a leg mean?"
"I don't know" Martin remarked casually.

"Should I not go back and ask him what he meant by that?"
"Naw" Martin said,
"leave him alone, it just gets him excited when you do things like that, we will just pretend we are keeping our eyes open for a leg."

As we walked around the head of the Prince of Wales dry dock we came across Eddie Connelly and his small squad of cobble stone layers repairing some broken cobble stones inside their little barriers in the middle of the road. Eddie saw us and shouted across, "Remember, Martin" and he stamped his right foot down hard on the roadway.
"use your foot on the bridge of everybody's nose to get a lift up the ladder of success in this life." Martin and I gave him a wave as we passed by.

"The man's a head case" Martin muttered,
"he says the same thing over and over again every time I pass him."

We reached the diving boat and climbed on board to find the lads feeding sprats to Jonathon. The bird was looking great, now that his grey and white plumage was beginning to grow steadily back towards its original size. Only his bottom was still bare, where the look-alike little arrows had fallen out, or, been torn out by himself in a rage of exasperation at their useless air lift ability.

"Where to this morning?" George asked, taking his attention away from Jonathon. The bird turned his head on one side and stared up at the sprat held loosely in George's right hand. Suddenly he leapt up from the bench seat, wings thrashing uselessly at the air in their attempt at lift, but he did manage to snatch the sprat out of George's hand. He gulped it down and stalked indignantly over to his box, stepped inside and settled down, resting his beak on the rim of the box.

"Imperial Dock" Martin answered.

"examining berths and we have to keep our eyes open for a leg."

"Whose leg?" George asked,

"No idea George, Grievie did not tell us whose leg it was.

"Are you having us on?" Andrew asked,

"No Andrew" I answered,

"I know it sounds crazy but that is exactly what David told us this morning, he said simply we were to keep our eyes open for a leg."

Jimmy Robertson had been cupping his ear to follow what was being said.

"It's the leg of that mate who went missing last month off the German ship." he said.

"How do you know that?" I asked loudly, so Jimmy would hear me.

"Because they got his body yesterday after it was blown to the surface by a ship's propeller and they reckon the prop had freshly cut one of his legs off."

"Where did you hear that?" Martin asked.

"Jock Wallace was telling everybody in the joiner shop this morning," Jimmy answered.

"he said the night the German went missing, he was spotted leaving Charlie's bar hopelessly drunk and must have fallen overboard and drowned himself."

"See" Martin said to me,

"Grievsie has trouble trying to explain things to us but you can always find out what is happening from Gabby mouth Wallace."

George started up the diving boat and took us out, and we locked into the Imperial Dock and Martin began dressing to make the dive.

The whole Port was buzzing with shipping at that time, and was as busy as it had ever been since the war ended. There were ships from the Ben Line, Furness-Withy, The Blair ships, The General Steam Navigation Company, the Ellerman Wilson Line, the North of Scotland Steam Navigation Company, and many of them were bulk carrying merchant ships with cargoes as varied as sulphur to Esparto grass and crates of whiskey to fruit and vegetables and cement.

There were oil rig supply vessels and ships delivering pipes to the firm of Bredero Price to be coated with concrete and used on the seabed to take the crude oil from the newly erected Oil Rigs to the shore. All the Bulk cargo vessels still kept the old fashioned Docker's system working. It would be some years yet before the invention of containers would sound the Death Knell on the Docker fraternity.

Martin dressed and went down and began sweeping half circles around the Dock floor to verify there were no obstructions that could damage a ship's hull. Meanwhile we threaded the diving boat in and out of the packed shipping lying alongside the quay walls. In the early afternoon Martin came up and stripped off the gear and to my amazement he informed us he was going for a walk along Seafield and would not be back on the boat, as he intended going straight to the diving hut after his walk.

He left the boat and I said,

"Suppose a special job comes up and we cannot get hold of him, what then?"

"Bobby" George said,

"he has done this for years and years and when a job does come up, we have to search all over for him."

"The big German bastard used to go missing for days at a time, when he was the only diver on the boat" said Andrew "and lucky enough to always get away with it."

"They say the Bosses were a bit nervous of him when he was younger, for he was a violent bugger." George said.

"That's how he got his bent nose." said Andrew,

"in a fight, and they had to patch it up using a bit of one of his own hip bones." He screwed his face up in distaste as he continued,

"He does not scare me, the big bent nosed German bastard." He stood up and flexed his shoulders.

"The good Lord gave me a good broad pair o' shooders," he then smiled at his own joke, for Andrew was a very small man and was as broad across his shoulders as a herring is between its eyes.

The sudden wailing of a siren brought us all out of the cabin to find out what was happening. An ambulance had drawn up beside the ship immediately in front of us and we could see quite a stir taking place among the Dockers on board. Andrew spotted his brother Henry among the Dockers and called out to him,

"What's going on Henry?"

Henry came up on the stern of the ship above us. He was as tall as Andrew was small and had large ears which jutted out on either side of his head, this was the reason the Dockers had nicknamed him 'The Scottish Cup.' He leaned over the ship's stern rail and said,
"One of our lads has just been crushed against the 'tween decks by a bale of Esparto grass coming up from the bottom of the hold and we think he is dead."

That evening I was to discover that Henry was right and the crushed Docker was indeed dead. The man was Robert Wylie and he and I had started primary school together at Craigentinny school at five years of age. We had also played in the same football team as twelve year olds. Many years later I was in the waiting room of Elsie Ingles Maternity hospital ready to greet my first born daughter, Hazel, and sat beside me was the same Robert Wylie also waiting to greet his first born child.

The following morning Martin and I were again in David's office at starting time.
"Same again Dave" Martin said,
"Right Martin, but eh!, are you remembering to eh! remembering to keep your eyes open for the eh! for the Leg."
"We have not forgotten David and we are looking for it all the time."
"Fine fine" said David, picking up his pen and lowering his head, his usual signal he was finished with us for now. As we rounded the dry dock we once more passed by the cobble stone laying squad working away inside their protective barriers. Eddie saw us coming and stamped his

right foot down on the cobbles and twisted it violently from side to side.

"Mind now Martin, that's everybody's face as a leg up to success in this life." he called across loudly.

"Head case" Martin muttered as we both smiled and waved back to Eddie. Back on the diving boat, which Martin and I had cleaned of Jonathan's droppings earlier that morning, we set off once more for the Imperial dock. Jonathan was in high spirits as he paddled furiously with both webbed feet on the bench seating, then gave Martin and I, as new arrivals, his wide open mouth signal. I had already given him a big feed first thing that morning so we ignored him. He stomped off towards his box in the corner of the compressor room and climbed in with his back facing us and huddled down, obviously in the huff because he was not offered more fish.

Back in the Imperial Dock, we tied up ahead of the grass boat in which poor Rab had perished the day before. I dressed and went down and began swinging around on the search line. I had no vision at all as I floundered through the thick silt, almost four feet deep in places. Around 2 pm in the afternoon Martin came on the diver phone,

"Bobby I am going to pick up my freshly laundered woollens so I will see you back at the hut at finishing time."

"Right Martin" I answered, but I thought to myself how can he do this, the stand-by diver is not supposed to leave the boat at all, while his buddy is submerged. I surfaced at 4 pm and the lads broke me out of the suit and prepared to take the diving boat back to her berth.

"Some stand-by diver" I said as I sipped the cup of coffee Jimmy had made me.

"It would be too easy to get snarled up down there among all the old mooring ropes and wires and discarded junk including pots and pans and prams and bikes and cars and kitchen sinks, the bottom of this Dock is like a huge rubbish Tip."
"That never bothers Martin," said Andrew,
"he is too thick in the head to recognise any kind of danger at all, yet up till now he has led a charmed life, the man has the luck of a pox doctor."
"I don't know what we would do if you did get trapped on the bottom while he was away for a walk, especially as far away as Seafield" said George.

I had a lot to think about, as I headed home that night. Uppermost in my mind was the thought that I must change my heretofore attitude of "Devil may care" whilst diving and be more careful in the future, I also decided I must find out from the lads why everybody kept warning me to keep Martin well away from my explosive Magazine.

Two days later I was again examining berths on the bottom of the Imperial Dock when I felt my search line snag on an obstruction, at the same time George came on the diver phone.
"You are going around something."
"Yes George I just felt it, I am closing in on it now." As I travelled in towards the centre of the search line I could feel the pull of a slight current on my body and the disturbed silt began clearing away rapidly around me. I realised the I.C.I. factory pumps were running and inducting water through their tunnels in the nearby cross berth. I continued in towards the snagged search line as the water cleared

completely and I could see my search line was caught up around the radiator of a motor car sitting upright on the bottom. When I reached it I saw the driver's window was fully down. I looked inside and found the car was empty.

"It's a motor car George, nobody in it fortunately, but you better get in touch with the yard and get them to send out Willie with his Neal's mobile crane to lift it out."

"Ok Bob will do" George answered.

"I'll come up for a coffee until the crane arrives, I'm starting back towards you now." I moved forward and stopped dead.

On the seabed in perfect view were two crabs feeding on the leg. Under normal diving conditions we would have certainly found the car but not the leg. The water intake tunnels had sucked all the disturbed silt away and given me extremely good visibility, otherwise I would never have seen it.

"Send me down a sugar sack George, I have found the leg."

"Sending you down a sugar sack shortly" George answered. I chased the crabs away from the leg and lay down to wait until George tied the sack on to my lines to send it down.

"Ok Bob take them down"

"Taking them down now," I brought my lines down hand over hand until the sack arrived and I untied it.

"Take up the slack George and stand by to bring me up."

"Taking up the slack."

I placed the leg in the bag while George was retrieving my loose lines, I felt George tighten up on me.

"Ready to take you away" he said and I spindled up with the leg.

Back on the boat with helmet and weights removed I looked for Jimmy with my expected cup of coffee, he was nowhere to be seen.

"Where is Jimmy?" I asked, Andrew gave a strange little laugh.

"He is away ashore, he said he does not mind when you bring up dead bodies but there is no way he is going to stay aboard when you are coming up with only a leg."

When the crane arrived I dressed again and returned to the bottom and slung the car, which was lifted up on to the quayside and left there while the Police examined it and also took away the leg.

Jimmy was still absent as we sailed back to our berth that night and George said,

"Funny how Jimmy did not seem to mind us bringing aboard the stinking body of the woman who committed suicide or the dead train driver and even the drowned Spanish sailor, yet he got in a right state and rushed ashore saying there was no way he was staying on board if you were bringing up just a leg on it's own."

Chapter 16

A Clean Sweep

We were back at our own berth in the early afternoon one day and Martin left us as usual. Jimmy passed out the coffee's and we settled down on the bench seating to relax and do nothing at all.
"Are you planning on fishing the top weir again on Saturday?" George asked.
"No, I was thinking of trying Amisfield again, Dad likes the bottom weir best of all and the fly fishing is good all the way up to Haddington."
"That's true and the golf course stretch lets us get at the water a lot easier than up at Pencaitland," George agreed.
I sat there thinking of the gentle flow of the river Tyne as it meandered through Haddington golf course, resembling at times a slow, deep canal.
 I thought back to one glorious summer's day when I had fished the same stretch of water, while George and Dad sat on the short grass behind me and watched my efforts. The sun blazed down out of a clear blue sky and a strong southerly wind was blowing downstream. All hopeless

conditions according to the ancient 'Boke of Saint Albans' wherein that worthy churchman stated

'The fyshings be not good when ther be a grett wind.' In sheer defiance of his theory, I used a dry fly to good account that day and landed twelve good trout in ten minutes, as witnessed by Dad and George.

A thought leapt into my head and I asked,
"Does Martin play golf?"
"No way," Andrew answered in a scornful tone of voice, "the only sport he is interested in, is tormenting his wife Martha."
"What do you mean tormenting his wife?" I asked.
"Bobby you have no idea what that poor lassie has to put up with, being married to Bendicks."
Although I would have preferred the conversation to continue revolving around the fishing, I was curious to know what Andrew meant so I asked,
"Such as what exactly?" and he told me the following story:

"Last year while he was on his holidays Grievsie asked me if I could deliver a note to him, because his house is close to mine and he never goes anywhere on holiday, so I took the note up to him, Martha opened the door to me and said,
"Oh! Come in Andrew, he is starting to paper the living room so just come through." I walked through with her and found Martin pasting the first piece of paper on his paste table.
"Hang on a minute Andrew until I get this first bit up and I will be right with you," he said. I noticed he had all the paper cut up into lengths lying in individual rolls at the end of his table.

He climbed up a step ladder with the first piece and applied the top of it to the wall and began smoothing out the air wrinkles, this done, he allowed the rest of the piece to drop downwards towards the floor. It finished up 8 inches above the skirting boarding. Martha looked at it and said,
"Oh! Martin you better stop for a minute." in a mild voice
"Don't bother me until I get this piece done," he shouted at her irritably.
"But I think you should stop for a minute" she said, looking up at him from the bottom of the ladder.
"WILL YOU WAIT JUST NOW" he roared, still smoothing out the top half of the paper.
"You better look at the bottom of it Martin" she said quietly.
"For God's sake woman will you be quiet?" he shouted but then he did look downwards.
  "He tore the paper off the wall and wrapped the pasted side of it around his wife's head and shoulders pressing it inwards into her face with both hands in his temper. What rational man carries on like that over a mistake he had made himself? He had cut all of the paper to the wrong size."
Andrew finished the story by exclaiming once again.
"God help the poor lassie, being married to that big bent nosed German bastard."

That same night as I was filling in my diving diary in the hut, Martin asked
"I wonder if you could do me a favour Bobby?"
"Certainly Martin if I can, what are you after?"
"I borrowed a set of plumber's rods along with a sweep's brush to clean my chimney from the bottom up but the brush became stuck pretty far up inside the flue and it's still

up there. I am not good at going up a height and although I live on the ground floor, the building I live in is four storeys high. Do you think you could go up on my roof and drop our shot weight down my chimney to get the brush out for me?"

"Ok Martin I will come with you tonight and clear it for you." At finishing time that evening, my Dad and Martin climbed into my car and I drove up Leith Walk. Dad came into Martin's house along with me and Martha had him sit down to a cup of coffee in their living room, while waiting on me completing the job.

While Martin was paying a quick visit to the toilet Martha whispered to me,

"The plumber put the brush on for him Boaby and told him he could work with it like that all the way up, but when he was ready to bring it down again he was to keep turning it clockwise all the time. He turned it the wrong way and unscrewed it and left the brush up there."

"So is the chimney clean?" I asked.

"Oh! Yes he got it completely clean before he tried to bring the brush down again."

I made my way up on to the roof of the building carrying our shot line made fast to our shot weight, which was a 4 inch diameter solid ball of pig iron. I called 'Halloo' down several pots until I had an answering call from Martin down below. Now sure of the right chimney, I lowered the shot weight down slowly and carefully until I felt it rest on the stuck brush, then raising it again about three feet I shouted down 'Stand Clear'and dropped the shot. Up out of the chimney came a roar of anguish.

When I returned to the ground I found Martin nursing an injured hand but he thanked me for recovering the brush for him so Dad and I left him and stopped off at our local on our way home for a beer and Dad told me the tiniest drop of soot came down the chimney when I gently landed the shot weight on the sweep's brush. Martin had grabbed hold of a small hand brush and shovel and although he heard me shout to stand clear he was still frantically trying to sweep up the morsel of soot when the shot weight thudded down onto the back of his hand.

The following morning I told the story to the rest of the diving team aboard our boat, while we were awaiting Martin's arrival. Not the least bit of sympathy was shown towards him, in fact, their attitude was tantamount to extreme glee over his misfortune.
"Serves him right" Andrew laughed outright,
"and I hope it gave Martha a laugh as well, although the poor lassie would probably be too scared to show it."
"I don't know how he ever managed to get Martha in the first place 'cos she's far too good natured to be lumbered wi' the like's o' him." Jimmy said sagely.
"You're right there Jimmy," George said,
"she must have the patience of a saint to put up with him."
The more I was finding out about Martin's nature, the more I was beginning to understand why the lads hated him so much.

Chapter 17

Martin's New Helmet

Every three months all our gear was tested and calibrated by our own Docks Commission engineers. We had to go off into deep water to have this done and the system involved first one diver going down and hanging off every ten feet in stages, all the way to the bottom, while his depth was manually checked against the actual reading on the gauges and then, if required, the gauges were altered accordingly.

Then the second diver followed suit and finally both together locked in a suggestive posture of legs and arms intertwined to keep both helmets' exhaust valves at exactly the same depth. In this manner it was up to the two linesmen to lower away together to each successive ten feet of depth until we reached the bottom. The engineer, Frank, always began with the diesel pump first, and checked its time to fill the two large storage cylinders mounted on either side of the boat, under the bench seating.

It was at the very start of the engineer's examination that the lorry arrived alongside Ranks mill, while we were having our lunch. It had a large packing case on board and this turned out to be Martin's new helmet. No child thrilling

over his Christmas presents ever enthused to the extent Martin did, over his new helmet. He lifted it out of its case with a reverence usually reserved for religious relicts, and laid it down on the bottom boards of the cabin. He ran his hands all over its gleaming brass work and shining copper and tinning, and while doing so he chuckled and laughed and crooned aloud, to the absolute disgust of Andrew watching him. Martin turned it over to look inside and the crooning and chuckling suddenly stopped.
"What the hell is that?" he asked of nobody in particular.

Andrew and George both looked inside the helmet and shrugged their shoulders together, Jimmy pretended not to hear by cupping a hand behind his deaf ear, as if he had missed what Martin had said. Frank, the engineer had a quick glance inside the helmet then said,
"You are the diver, if you don't know Martin, how are we supposed to know." I moved closer to see what Martin was talking about and said,
"That's a knock valve, you sure have a modern helmet now Martin."
"What the hell is a knock valve?" he asked,
"I don't want a knock valve, I don't want it, whatever the hell it is," he added peevishly and all his exuberance evaporated instantly.
"That's fine Martin" I said,
"I will take it, it's a real beauty of a helmet."

Martin threw his arms around the helmet and dragged it towards him and away from me.
"Oh! No you won't, its mine and I'm changing over to it right now." In all my life I never met another man who could change moods faster than Martin Bendicks could.

In the afternoon I was first to make the solo dive and have my gear checked by Frank the engineer. Having successfully calibrated my gauges, Frank had me come aboard and Martin dressed ready to make his first dive in his new helmet. Still dressed, I moved into the cabin, out of the way. Martin gripped the shot line and stepped off the ladder and there he floated, high and handsome, alongside the boat.
"I can't go down" he said, in a voice loaded with wonder and amazement at the fact he remained floating with his shoulders almost fully out of the water altogether.
"I can't go down," he repeated over the phone. George and Andrew both looked at me questioningly, I could not stop myself from laughing and they both started laughing with me as Martin again repeated.
"I can't go down George," In a tone indicative of sheer amazement. George looked at me and said,
"What do I say to him?"
"Ask him why he can't go down"
"Why can't you go down Martin?"
"How the fuck should I know?" Martin shouted in a fit of instant rage,
"this fucking helmet won't let me sink." He was becoming overly excited so I decided to calm him down, I moved over to the phone.
"Martin push the knock valve with your head and you will sink instantly" he did not answer me, but he obviously operated the knock valve and away down he went.
"Martin" I added,
"when you spindle back up, you will have to use the knock valve again." I fully expected him to ask why, but there

being no answer from him, I gave up, thinking to myself any normal man would surely at least ask what I meant, if he failed to understand what had been said to him, but not Martin. Frank began his calibration of Martin's gauges and as the diver was dropping each of his ten foot stops, I had plenty time to warn the two linesmen of what was about to happen.

"You see lads, it is a physical impossibility to bring about a true neutral buoyancy in a helmet. It either gains buoyancy or loses it, no matter how finely you set your exhaust valve. Now, when you are working in mid water, you want your helmet floating just clear of your shoulders and no more, so you set your spindle valve to give that result. This means very, very slowly you are inflating all the time. The knock valve is designed to assist you to lose the extra air without having to use your hands to adjust the exhaust valve. You simply press the knock valve with your head and the helmet spills all the excess air and begins once again to start slowly inflating from scratch."

"I see what you mean" George said, while Andrew admitted he had never seen a knock valve before, or ever heard of one, in all his long years as a linesman.

"When Martin has finished his dive and attempts to spindle up, like he has done all his diving days, he will probably not head the knock valve which means he will lose control of his suit and bullet up from the bottom. His suit will become bloated and as hard as a rubber tyre with pressure and that is where the danger lies. If he blows a cuff on the way up he will sink faster than a stone. So you lads must bring his lines in, as fast as is humanly possible, to stop him from free falling to the bottom if a cuff does go, otherwise we will have a dead diver on our hands."

"Why do you think he will lose control?" Andrew asked.

"Because if he does not head the valve, his suit will expand faster than he has ever known it do before. I tried to tell him but it seems he does not like to be told how to do anything at all and that means he WILL blow up out of control."

While we were talking two swans came wheeling in out of a clear sky. They skidded to a halt on the surface, not very far from our boat, at the same time Frank said he was finished and Martin's gauges were now calibrated correctly, so he told George he could now bring Martin up. The two swans had noticed Martin's bubbles erupting on the surface and they began to paddle over to them, to investigate what they were.

"That's it Martin" George said,

"Frank says you can come up now."

"Ok George take up my slack." The two swans had reached the bubbles and were paddling around in a circle in the very centre of them. They had their heads cocked to one side in curiosity over this strange phenomenon.

"Take me away" Martin called and the two linesmen brought the lines in smartly hand over hand.

Over the phone came a long drawn out wail of fear increasing in volume all the time.

"aaaaaaaaAAAAA AAAHHHHHHHHH!" and Martin exploded out of the water as high as his knees and crashed over backwards to lie floating, as high as an inflatable mattress. The two swans had been swept upwards out of the water along with him and then landed back on his chest, with all four wings beating the air in a frantic effort to escape the grotesque monster that they thought was attacking them.

The lads towed Martin over to the boat and George leaned over and gripped the elbow of his air hose connection with one hand and lifted slightly, he also tried to spin open the exhaust valve with his other hand, only to find it was already wide open. Martin lay spreadeagled on the surface with arms and legs swollen to a ridiculous degree and with no sign of the air leaving his suit. He was also strangely silent on the phone,
"Are you ok, Martin?" I asked.
"I'm ok but this bloody helmet refuses to let any air go at all," he said bitterly.
"Martin, push the knock valve with your head." At last he did what I said and his boots slowly sank down and he turned vertical and climbed up the ladder and George removed his helmet. Other than looking a bit pale with the fright, Martin seemed to be none the worse for his first encounter with his new helmet.

After he had recovered somewhat we both dressed and entered the water together and wrapped our arms and legs around each other as we floated beside the boat.
"Right Martin if you will head your knock valve we will both sink and I will say no more and you can take it from here down," I said, leaving Martin to do all the talking.
"Ok Lads" Martin said as he spilled air by heading the valve,
"down to the first stop slowly."

Hanging there at our first stop at ten feet under the boat, I looked out through my right side light at the shafts of sunlight coming down from the surface and illuminating the greeny-blue of the sea water.

"Ok Martin, Frank has finished, we are ready to lower you both to the next stop," said George.

"Lower away" Martin said and I marvelled at the subtle changes taking place in the shades of colour as we dropped.

I was now looking out at a slightly darker aquamarine blue. Martin's left arm rested around my shoulders and I noticed the translucent brightness of green was still showing locally on his forearm in patches, as seen through the larger of my exhaust bubbles as they appeared to accentuate and magnify the remaining light and focus it on Martin's arm.

"Down again Martin" said George,

"Ok down gently" Martin agreed. Now thirty feet deep, everything changed to a slate grey/blue, except again when viewed through the bubbles, small areas of Martin's arm and hand retained the lighter colour of the previous stop. It was not until we were below forty feet, that everything changed to a very dark ultra marine blue. Yet again my exhaust bubbles appeared to be adding light to parts of Martin's arm and hand, which gave them a much brighter hue than the rest of their surroundings.

As we carried on down to greater depths this property of the bubbles appeared to vanish altogether as they took the form of quicksilver globules, shining like streams of large pearls as they headed upwards towards the surface. Martin was none the worse for his first run-in with his new helmet and the two swans were also uninjured in the melee, and were last seen flying strongly in a northerly direction. I felt they must have considered they were lucky to have escaped from, what they possibly thought of, as 'A land where there be Giants.'

Chapter 18

The Chippers

A corvette sat on the chocks in the bottom of the Alexandra dry dock while a small squad of Chippers applied coat after coat of red lead paint to her hull. They worked for Henry Robb's shipyard and they had the meanest and dirtiest job in all of Dockland. They were the men who scraped all the marine growth of barnacles and mussels off the ship's bottom and chipped away any rust that was forming, before liberally applying the red lead paint.

They were unconcerned that their rollers continually spattered the paint over them, as they worked away, it was almost impossible to detect any of the original white material of their Boiler suits. They were all very small men, not one of them stood more than 5 foot three inches tall, but what they lacked in inches they more than made up for in wit, and they were extremely funny. They kept up a pretended animosity towards each other, with a never ending banter as they worked away.

Shovel Chin Ritchie thrust out his prominent lower jaw even further than usual, as he applied his roller to the ship's bottom. "You niver fought the Jerries in the war," he said with some conviction.

"Whey didnae, ah most certainly did" said Tucker

"Where aboot did you fight them then?" asked Shovel Chin in a sarcastic, disbelieving voice as he glared at Tucker.

"In Belgium and France" Tucker replied indignantly, as he turned his roller sideways in slow circles to stop it dripping red lead paint on the floor of the dock.

"Aye that'll be right" wee Smithy called, emerging from behind one of the chocks that the ship sat on.

"You ran awa' frae the Jerries, through baith Belgium and France, aw' the wye tae Dunkirk."

"Aye" Tucker agreed,

"we had tae run tae stert wi', 'cos the Jerries had aw' the guns an' bullets an' Tanks an' fings. Run? ye ken yon big Belgium hares wi' the long back legs an' the sticky up ears, well ah wis bootin' them oot o' ma road shoutin' ah'll show ye somebody that kin run."

"Oh! Gawd" said Shovel Chin screwing up his face and turning his eyes up to the sky, as if imploring the heavens for some divine aid.

Tucker ignored him as he carried on,

"But when they gave us aw' the guns an' bullets an' Tanks and fings, we chased the Jerries aw' the wye back tae Germany oot o' trench efter trench." He pulled a cloth out of his top pocket and wiped away a splash of red paint from his face.

"So that's where you wur hidin' " Wee Smithy said, again emerging from behind the chock,

"in the trenches."

"You think ah wis hidin' dae ye? well ah'll tell ye, wan day a sergeant came along and shouted doon,
"Is there a guy called Tucker in that trench?"
"Ma name is Tucker sergeant," ah answered.
"Come up here" he said, "fur you ur in soapy bubble ma lad, there is a General here tae see you."
"Help ma Boab" said Shovel Chin,
"no less than a General himsel' tae see him. It couldna be a Captain nor a Major, it hud tae be a full GENERAL." He cast his eyes heavenwards once more.
"aw! hud yer tongue" said Tucker, feigning anger and threatening Shovel chin with his roller held on high, before spinning it dexterously and setting it in motion once more against the ship's bottom.
"Anywye ah climbed oot o' the trench an' stood tae attention wi' ma rifle oan ma shooder an' this General came along an' said,
"Is your name Tucker?" an' ah said "Yes Sir" an' he said,
"I huv been sent ower here aw' the wye from the U.K. specially tae get a haud o' you an' stoap yer shenanigans cause you ur nothin' but a menace.

You huv goat the war department in some bloody state, dae you not realise they had planned this war tae last for four and a half years, but the rate you are killin' they Jerries at, it will be lucky if it lasts fur any mair than four and a half months, and forbye that, you ur the untidiest soldier in the British army."

"Ah sterted tryin' tae rub the mud aff ma knees thinking that's whit he meant, fur the trenches were awfy muddy at that time but he roared at me."
"Look at yer rifle man," an' when ah turned ma heid an'

looked up at ma gun, there was a deid Jerry hingin' oan ma bayonet." Shovel chin groaned in a deep voice saying,
"If ever a man suffered, am sufferin' this day havin' tae listen tae aw' this drivel."
Wee Willie Velzine called across from under the ship's port side
"How did ye manage tae reach up high enough tae bayonet a jerry fae your wee height?"

His strong Polish accent made the Scottish slang words sound so comical.
Wee Smithy popped out from behind the chock once again.
"He heid butted them in thir knees furst, tae bring them doon tae his level," he said, laughing loudly at his own joke.
"Heh! Velzine, ah thocht you said you wur a prisoner o' the Jerries yersel' said Tucker,
"so how did ye manage tae escape?"

"That's right, ah wis a prisoner, an' they took me oan a train tae wurk in France, but when the train stoapped at a station ah ran awa' intae the wids, even though a guard wis watchin' me at the time."
"He widna ken ye were a man, an' probably thocht it wis jist a wee field moose running awa intae the trees" said Tucker.

The Polish expatriate ignored him and carried on,
"Ah wis stervin' efter a while, wi' naethin' tae eat in the wids so ah went doon tae a French fairm an' asked the fairmer's wife fur somethin' tae eat. She let oot a scream an' hur man came effter me wi' a shotgun."
"Whit fur did he dae that ?" wee Smithy asked
"Well ah fund oot later, when ah asked hur fur somethin' tae eat in Polish, 'cos ah no speak ony French, but in French she

think ah askin' if ah could shag her, an' hur man no seem tae like that, an' he try tae blaw ma heid aff wi' a shotgun."

"Fur Gawds sake it gets worse by the minute," Shovel chin Ritchie complained,
"is there no limit tae you's guy's imagination?"
Tucker then sang out loudly,
"Hey! Wullie, when you lived in Poland afore the war, wur you ever a Lion tamer?"
"Naw niver, whit fur dae ye ask that?"
"Cos noo adays you ur nothin' but a lyin' little bastard" said Tucker, allowing himself a faint grin at wee Smithy's explosive howl of laughter.

The Chipper's antics and stories kept Martin and I amused as we plugged leaks on the inside of the Dry Dock gates by caulking them from the bottom up, using soft wood tiddler wedges. We did this wearing just the diving suits by themselves, with the bibs tied up around our necks, to keep us reasonably dry. The continual use of the dry dock meant we could not get a chance to dive and renew the proper seals on the outside of the gates when they were open.

Small leaks could be plugged from the outside, with the gates closed, by dropping fly ash down the back of them which was sucked into the mitre and the quoins by the pressure, but any larger leaks just sent the fly ash right through into the Dock.

To look at wee Smithy, plastered from head to toe in red lead paint at his work, you could never imagine the change in him that would take place when he would go off at night to the Old Time Dancing in the El Dorado Ballroom.

Immaculately clean and wearing a tailored evening dress suit and bow tie, with shiny black patent dancing shoes on his feet and his sparse fair hair neatly groomed and Brylcreemed into place, and even Cinderella herself could not have bettered his transformation into a proper little dandy. It was a pity his speech could not match the rest of his image.

"Last night ah went up tae this luverly girl and said tae hur would you like for to dance with me, an' she said ah wid luv for to dance with you, so we did the Tango."

"The Tango eh!" Shovel chin remarked,

"so you wur oot tanglin' wi' the lassies o' Leith last night wur ye."

"Aye, the Tango, an' she said tae me, you dance divinely, jist like George Raft."

"Ur ye sure the girl hersel' wisnae George Raft, if she fell fur the likes o' you?" asked Tucker.

"Shut yer face," wee Smithy shouted over angrily,

"It's you that's the daft yin, she was a proper lady an' she said to me, you dance divinely and I would like you for to be ma felly." Willie Velzine then called across,

"If she wants you fur hur felly she must be George Raft right enough." Wee Smithy glared out from behind the chock at him as he said,

"We ur gonny get merrit next year." Shovel chin turned his eyes up to the heavens once again saying,

"Gawd help the poor lassie if she feeneshes up merrit tae the likes o' you."

Martin came shuffling back from the far end of the Dock carrying a twelve foot long timber ladder.

"Can you foot the ladder for me so I can get higher up the mitre?" he asked.

"Right Martin," I agreed, following him up on to the sill and wading through three feet of water coming from the leaking gates. He placed the ladder well up the mitre and climbed up with a bag of tiddler wedges. I set both feet against the bottom of the stringers and took hold of the ladder with both hands at shoulder height. He was doing fine all the way up, until he tried to reach over to a leak which was really too far away from him. He lost his balance and fell sideways with both feet still on the ladder.

He grabbed hold of the near side stringer and frantically tried to tug his body upright. The ladder began sliding side on down the slimy green face of the gates and although I threw my body weight in the opposite direction trying to stop it, I had no chance with Martin's weight pulling it over from the top and both the ladder and Martin came crashing down into four feet of water over the trinket at the bottom of the sill. He plunged under head first and surfaced gasping as he scrambled out of the trinket and bent over tugging at his bib with both hands trying to empty the water out of it.

"Why the hell did you not catch me?" he yelled at me angrily.
"Don't be stupid" I shouted back,
"if I weighed twenty stone, I still could not hold back your weight cantilevering side on at the top of a twelve foot long ladder."

For once we were providing entertainment for the Chippers instead of the reverse. They found the whole incident extremely funny, and to Martin's discomfort they laughed loud and long at him as he coughed and spat out the sea, still bending over and trying to pour the remaining water out of his suit. In the end he gave up and informed me he was going up to the hut to change and he would not be back.

Apparently he did not care that I was left to complete the job on my own, with nobody to foot the ladder for me. I carried on very carefully up the mitre and the small softwood tiddler wedges soon began swelling up and reduced the leaks to a dribble of water. This meant the Pump-house man did not have to keep constantly starting and stopping his pumps, so that the men working under the ship could remain comfortably dry.

As soon as Martin left the Dock the Chippers were at it again.

"Aw! C'moan" said Shovel chin Richie,

"ur ye askin' us tae believe you were auld enough tae fight in the furst Wurld War as well, when were ye boarn anywye?"

Tucker mimicked the out thrust of Shovel chin's lower jaw and slurping speech as he answered.

"Ah wis boarn oan the umpteenth o' September nineteen oat cake, so ye see wise guy, ah wis auld enough, but ah didnae go in the end"

"Whit fur did ye no go in the end?" Willie Velzine asked gruffly.

"Cos his Mother was tell't tae get his pram aff the bloody battlefield" said wee Smithy, who was the only one in the squad who laughed at his own jokes, the others delivered their stories with dead pan faces.

"Very funny, heh! heh! heh! "said Tucker, mimicking wee Smithy's laughing giggle almost perfectly.
"naw it wis because ah tell't them ah wis a semiconscious subjective."
"Ye mean a conscientious objector" Shovel chin corrected him derisively.
"Aye, an' ah tell't them ah wis that as well, jist fur guid meesure" said the unflustered wee man.
"Well, how did ye get oan?" Shovel chin asked.
"Ah goat the Jile fur refusin' tae fight."
"They locked ye up in the jile did they?" wee Smithy asked.
"Aye, an' they tell't me ah hud tae take a baff, so ah hud tae take aw' ma claes aff an' huv a baff."
  "Help ma Boab that must have been a horrific experience fur ye," said Shovel chin, shuddering, and pretending to be shocked and thoroughly alarmed at the dire treatment his workmate had suffered. Tucker ignored the insinuation that he and a bath were rank strangers to each other.
"Then they gave me an arrer suit tae pit oan."
"Whit iss an arrer suit?" asked Willie Velzine.
"See you Poles, you ur awfy stupit, an arrer suit is wan that looks like a burd has walked through a pot o' black paint an' then walked aw' ower the suit an' left loads o' wee arrers aw' ower it, so that everybody kens you ur a convict. Then they locked me in a cell."
  "Whit did ye dae,?" asked wee Smithy, forgetting to use his usual badinage against Tucker, in his desire to hear the rest of the tale.
"Whit could ah dae, ah jist sat there, then ah thocht ah'll hae a wee smoke." Shovel chin leapt in.

"Ah thocht you said they took yer claes away, where did ye get the fags fae?".

"You should shut that big mooth o' yours," yelled wee Smithy, who was desperate to hear the end of the story.

"They did take ma claes away but ah hud half a fag behind ma right ear an' wan match ahint ma left ear."

"But ye said they made ye take a baff," said Shovel chin triumphantly, as if he had finally cornered Tucker in a lie. Wee Smithy lost his rag completely.

"If you don't shut yer face ah'll empy this tray o' red leed ower yer heid." Shovel chin blinked and turned his head away from the threat as Tucker carried on,

"They did make me take a baff but ah niver goat ma heid wet."

"How could ye tak a baff withoot gettin' yer heid wet?" Willie Velzine sneered contemptuously. Wee Smithy turned on him viciously

"An' you can shut up an aw', ya wee Polish scunner." he screamed. Tucker actually smiled at the havoc his story was causing among the members of the little squad.

"So ah wis sittin' there enjoyin' ma smoke when ah noticed an eye lookin' at me through a wee peephole in the cell door an' a voice suddenly roared oot.

"Oho! you ur in soapy bubble ma lad, smoking eh!, you ur gaun tae see the Governor.

Two great big guys came in an'grabbed me an' marched me aff tae the Governor's Office an' they tell't him ah hud smuggled tabacca intae the prison, the lyin' bastards didnae say it wis only a wee fag end. The Governor goat really nasty sayin' it wis a very serious crime, smugglin' tabacca intae wan o' his Majestie's prisons, an' so ah asked him if ah could explain whit happened, an' ah spent the next twalve' meenits an' tell't him aw' aboot the wee fag end an' the wan match an' a' that, and dae ye ken whit he said?"

Wee Smithy had been listening avidly, his breathing coming and going audibly out of his half open mouth, he gulped to hurriedly close it, so he could ask,

"Whit did he say, whit did he say?"
"He tell't his twa muckle thugs he hudna a clue whit ah wis ravin' aboot an' he sentenced me to 14 days solitary confinement oan nothin' but breed an'water. The furst day a big guy came intae ma cell wi' a chunk o' stale breed and a tin mug fu' o' water an' ah frew it aw' aboot him."

I had listened to the whole story without any comment whatsoever but I could not resist the temptation at the finish to ask Tucker.
"And did you throw it all about him on the last day of your sentence?"
"Did ah hell" he said vehemently, "cos ah could huv ett the guy that brung it in."

One week later I was sitting in the little coffee shop just outside Sandport Street Gate, four inches of snow lay on the pavement and a blizzard was blowing outside the front windows of the shop. Three inches of thick ice lay on the water of the Old Dock nearby and by God it was cold. I spotted the small rotund figure of Tucker coming towards the shop draped in an enormous overcoat, which hid his feet altogether and dragged along through the snow behind him. The lapels were turned up over his ears and his nose was sporting a rather rich colour of purple beneath the cloth cap on his head and his hands were dug deep in the large pockets of the coat. The girl behind the counter watched him enter the shop,

"Oh! Tucker son, you look absolutely frozen, would you like a steamin' hoat cup o' coffee?" she asked.

"Aye thanks hen" the little comedian answered,

"jist fro it aw aboot me."

The girl smiled as she poured him his coffee from a large urn.

"It's awfy cauld today isn't it Tucker son?" she said pleasantly.

"Aye hen" Tucker agreed, blowing on his bare fingertips sticking out of the ends of a pair of small mittens.

"But it's no' as cauld as it might have been, if it had been a lot caulder than it is," he said solemnly. The girl's brow wrinkled as she tried to work out exactly what the little man was saying, then giving up, she shook her head and handed him his coffee.

He came over carrying his mug and sat down at the next table to me.

"Hi! There Boab, that wis an awfy state Bendicks goat hissel' in ower getting a wee bit wet in the Alex last week," he said clasping both hands around the mug of hot coffee.

"I think he was more upset because you chippers were laughing at him."

"Wis it any wonder we laughed at him, a DIVER, complainin' he had goat hissel' a wee bit wet, aw! C'moan Boab." He grinned at me as he slurped down the hot coffee, then glanced up at the shop's clock, hanging on the wall behind the counter.

"Haulf past free," he remarked, turning back towards me with an amazed, concerned look on his face,
"is that aw' the time it is already, ah better hurry back afore ah'm missed, but did ye ken he fell oot wi' me last year?" he asked confidentially.
"How come?"
"He came oot the diving hut jist as ah wis gaun ower the swing bridge an he shouted ower tae me. Hey! Tucker did you hear the result o' the Derby?" an ah said.
"Oh! Aye, ah did, eh!, whit-dae-ye-call-it wis furst, and eh! whit's-its-name-again wis saicant, but ah huv nae idea whit wis third. Ah'll tell ye Boab, he looked like he hud goat hissel' angry enough tae stert rippin' up burnt paper an' he certainly wisna very happy wi' me at aw"

Chapter 19

Gibson Heirs Foreman

It was 9 o clock on a friday night and I had just finished loading all my fishing gear into the boot of my car and was about to leave home and pick up my Dad for an all night fishing trip. Another five minutes and I would have been clear to go, alas it was not to be. Mabel called from the house telling me a 'phone call had just come through and I must go back down to the Docks right away. She said a van had driven over the quayside into the Edinburgh Dock with the driver still in it.

Cursing my luck I drove down to Dad's house to let him know the trip was off, then set out for Leith. The police officers on duty at Constitution Street Gate waved me down as I tried to enter the Docks. This was unusual, they normally would only occasionally stop and search men and vehicles leaving the Docks, never entering them.

A sergeant came towards me as I slowed down but he must have recognised my maroon and ascot grey Ford Zodiac for he waved me through before I reached him.

It was extremely dark and strangely silent as I drove alongside the dim outline of the cargo sheds by the

Quayside and for a few moments my main beam headlight fell on a fox pursuing his nocturnal hunting of the many rabbits which also inhabited Dockland. I drew up in front of the diving hut to find I was the first to arrive. Opening up the front door and switching on all the lights, I then gathered up all of our clean woollens and loaded them into two large kit bags and set off round to the boat.

I jumped on board and opened the cabin door and switched on all the boats lights. Jonathan watched me as I closed the blow down valves of our compressor and began re-fuelling the diving pump, but for once he failed to come out of his box to greet me. If anything, he appeared to cower down lower in his box, as if a sense of foreboding had overtaken him. The bird's reaction caused me to ponder over the old saying that seagulls carried the souls of drowned men with them and as I watched him, I felt an eerie sensation that somehow the bird felt the presence of a recently released soul.

George was next to arrive, carrying two dry diving suits which he threw on the cabin top before jumping on board, he looked as upset as I was at a Friday night call out and proved it by saying.
"I was looking forward to tonight's episode of Rawhide on the Telly when the bloody messenger arrived. The last thing I wanted was to come back down here, but I ran into big Andy, the Dock Deputy coming off duty and he told me about the van going into the Dock. He said the driver of the van never got out of it before it sank."

"How did he know that?" I asked.
"He was around at the Roll-on, Roll-off boat which was leaving for Rotterdam and it had just left the quayside when

the van went in at the cross berth in front of the Mill and started drifting out towards the ship. The crew had time to lower a dinghy and row over to it, but by the time they reached it, only the van's roof was showing on the surface and they were unable to prevent it sinking. They told Andy there was no sign of the driver."

"If it took as long as that to go down it is possible the driver did get out of it."

"No, the crew of the Ro-Ro ship were positive no one came out of it."

The sound of voices on the quayside announced the arrival of Andrew and Jimmy and with them on board we set off for the Imperial Lock without waiting for Martin. We knew he would be walking down from his house in Leith Walk, as he no longer used his bicycle and had never owned a car. The neap tide was pretty low and we arrived at the lock to see the Ro-Ro ship leave and set sail for Rotterdam. She had such a shallow draft she could sail at almost any stage of a neap tide.

We entered the lock ready to be lifted up to Harbour level and above us on the quayside we could see Martin waiting to come on board. The lock filled and Martin joined us, as we set sail for the Edinburgh's east end cross berth. A slight mist added to the darkness of the night and blurred the lights of the moored ships as we sailed past their ghostly forms. It was bitterly cold and for once I was quite happy that it was Martin's turn to make the dive.

At the far end of the Edinburgh Dock we could see a greater concentration of lights emerging from the thickening fog which was beginning to wrap itself around us. As we closed the distance, we saw these lights came from Police cars, an Ambulance, a fire engine and several ordinary cars, all with their headlights trained on the surface of the water.

We came alongside the cross berth and two C.I.D. men waiting there intimated they wished to come on board our boat. We picked them up from the stone steps at the end of the quay and they directed us back out towards the centre of the Dock, where we could now see engine oil erupting on the surface. George began dressing Martin in the cabin while Jimmy, Andrew and I positioned our boat in the centre of the pool of oil which was continuing to bubble up from the depths below us.

We then anchored the boat and dropped the shot line over the side and secured it to the diving ladder.
Martin stepped out on to the ladder to finish dressing and the detectives wanted to have a word with him before his helmet went over his head.
"If you find anyone down there don't touch them until we tell you what we want you to do first," one of the detectives said.
"I take it we can speak to you when you are on the bottom?"
"Yes you can speak to me over the diver phone." Martin answered.
"Tell us what you find down there but don't move anything at all until we tell you to do so, we might need you to describe what you find first, before moving anything,"
"Right" Martin agreed,
"can I put my helmet on now?"
The detectives stood back and one said,
"Ok diver you can carry on." George finished dressing him and slapped the top of the helmet.

Martin slipped off the ladder and sank quickly into the dark freezing water of the Dock.

"On the bottom" he reported,

"You are on the bottom" George replied over the phone.

The two Detectives stood either side of George and stared at the diver phone as if fascinated by the sound of Martin's bubbles coming from it, then his voice.

"The van is sitting upright on it's wheels but it has sunk well down into the silt, I can see inside it and there is nobody in the driver or passenger seats."

"Right Martin," George answered. A few minutes went by in silence then Martin spoke again,

"I am now round at the back doors but I can't see anything through the windows, do you want me to try and open the back doors?"

"Tell him to go ahead and open the doors but don't touch anything else."

"Ok Martin you can open up the doors but don't touch anything other than the doors," George told him. Now there was a long delay and one detective asked,

"What is he doing now?"

"What's happening Martin?" George asked.

"I am having to dig the silt away from the back doors before I can get them open," Martin answered. One of the detectives turned to me and asked,

"How deep is the mud on the bottom down there?"

"It can be anything from two to four feet deep, depending on how many ships have recently been moving above it and disturbing it."

"Oh! as much as that," they were not very talkative so I tried to draw them out by asking,

"Have you any idea who might have been driving that van tonight?"

"We are not sure at the moment but it may have been Gibson Heirs Foreman Plumber," one of them said.

"We got a report he was drinking quite heavily in Granton earlier on tonight and when he climbed in his van he collided with a parked car in Granton Square, but he was spotted doing so by one of our ordinary Panda cars travelling in the opposite direction. By the time the Police Panda got itself turned around to go after him, he had taken off at speed towards Leith.

The Police on the Dock gates then reported a Van going past them driving recklessly at speed and finally one of the Dock Deputies saw a van try to turn in front of the grain Elevator but it was going so fast it never completed the turn before it flew off the quayside into the Dock."

In an excited voice Martin came back on the diver phone.
"I got the back doors open and a drowned man fell out into my arms."
"Fell out into his arms, ask him how come?" said one of the detectives, as if he found such a thing suspicious.
"How did that happen Martin?" George asked,
"It looks like he must have been tearing at the doors with his fingernails, which are all broken and then he must have slumped against the doors and drowned when they would not open. He was leaning against them and just fell out."
"Ok" said the first detective,
"just tell your diver to bring him up."
"Martin" George said,
"the Police Officers want you to bring the man up."

"Right George take up my lines and take me away." Martin bounced on to the surface with the dead man and we towed them over to the boat and pulled the body on board. We sailed back to the Quay and delivered the drowned man to the waiting Ambulance men and the two detectives went with him.

We had it confirmed later that it was Gibson Heirs Foreman Plumber, just as the C.I.D. men had suspected. We set off sailing back to our own berth while I found my thoughts beginning to compare some of the tragic deaths our work involved us in.

The young plumber foreman drinking and driving, which was not an offence in itself at that time and only became an offence if a person caused an accident while doing so. The frightened young man must have panicked, probably seeing the Panda car trying to turn and come after him, so he had sped away at speed to his premature death.

The middle aged Prostitute who hated her life so much she deliberately ended it, by jumping from Bernard Street bridge.

The Train driver who had a heart attack and drove his train into the Dock.

The young Prostitute on board a small coaster at 3 a.m. in the morning, who decided to jump ashore, instead of using the ship's Gangway. She stumbled and fell between the ship and the quay and might have survived if our tugs had not been passing at the time, unfortunately they were and the wash of their propellers caused the ship to crush her against the stone quay and drown her.

The 26 year old Spanish sailor, Angel Gonzalez, Gonzalez drowning in broad daylight, in flat calm water, because he had never learned to swim.

The German First Officer, too drunk to get safely back on board and whose leg was missing for a while.

The office workers of the firm of Fisons, three girls and a man, who were in a car driving through the Docks on their way home in thick fog and missed the Passageway Bridge and rolled over the edge of the quay, they all drowned,

Bill Riddle, the Pumphouse man who accidentally reversed his car down into his own Alexandra Dry Dock.

The Docker, Robert Wylie crushed against the 'tween decks by a bale of Esparto grass coming up from the hold below him

So many different circumstances surrounded these unfortunate accidents, but they all ended in the tragic demise of all of the participants.

Chapter 20

The YO-YO

"Same as yesterday, Davy," Martin said that morning.
"renewing the rubber seals on the Edinburgh dry dock gates."
"NO no Martin" David Grieve said, forgetting to lay down his pen.
"the Boatmen have lost their eh!, lost their boat the Yo-Yo, you have to go and eh!, have to go and help them to find it."
"Right Davy, we will go and help the Boatmen to find the Yo-Yo" Martin said, in what to me sounded like a placating tone of voice, as if he expected a sudden outburst from our easily irritable Works Manager at any time and he was trying his best to prevent that from happening.

As we walked away towards the diving hut Martin asked "Do you know any of the Boatmen Bobby?"
"I know Arthur and George Peebles, they both served their time before I did in Henry Robb's Joiner shop."
"Yes" Martin agreed,
"the Peebles family have a long history as Boatmen."

Like ourselves the Boatmen provided a Port service, although they remained independent of the Commission's direct control. The need for their services began away back in the days when motive power of shipping relied on sails and wind alone. At present they attended each ship's arrival or departure and with their motor launch the Yo-Yo, they would either ferry mooring ropes out to the large buoys in the centre of each Dock which enabled ships leaving to warp themselves away from the quayside by using their own steam winches, or they would ferry wires and ropes from the ships arriving, to the shore so they could winch themselves alongside the quays. Like trawler men, the Boatmen kept it 'in the family' so to speak. It was a closed shop unless your Great-Great-Grandfather had also been a Boatman.

Change however, was already beginning to come about which would bring an end to this ancient profession. Some oil supply vessels were now arriving fitted with the new bow thrusts, which allowed them to berth without any assistance.
"Where to this morning?" George asked as Martin and I jumped aboard.
"Back to the Edinburgh dry dock is it?"
"No George, round to the Boatman's offices," said Martin.
"they have lost the Yo-Yo."

I took the helm and we set off, the lads started up the diving compressor and I was instantly joined on the stern of the boat by Jonathan. He looked magnificent and stood tall and proudly thrust out his milk white chest, the grey of his nearly fully formed plumage on his back and upper wing surfaces shone with a lustre that only a healthy well fed gull could possess.

He turned his head on one side and I thought he was eyeing me up and down, but I was wrong. He was actually gauging the height from the stern sheets to the top of the cabin. He suddenly spread his wings and lifted off the transom and with his bare bum hanging very low under him, he beat the air furiously with his wings and rose just high enough to manage a rather ungainly crash landing on top of the cabin roof. He scrambled back on his feet again and glared reproachfully over his back at me, as if the belated attempt at a landing was all my fault.

I was wrong in this assumption as well, because he began pecking at his own bare bum rather viciously and was obviously blaming it, for it's lack of air lift during his short flight.

Overhead we were joined by some of his own kind flying above us and Jonathan turned his attention to them. The slight breeze blowing towards us was intensified by our forward motion into it and Jonathan spread his wings once more but only to hold his balance. He made no attempt to take off and join his fellow gulls flying above us.

We arrived at the Imperial basin to find Arthur Peebles waiting on the quayside and talking to Willie Kerr, who was sitting inside his mobile Neals crane. The crane had two spreader bars with belly wires hanging from them under it's hook, so it seemed they must have been pretty sure the Yo-Yo had sunk.

"Martin," Arthur called when we were close enough to hear him.
"we reckon she is on the bottom beside the quay."
"What makes you think that?" Martin called back.

"We were told some young lads were aboard her and must have pulled out the spile and let go her moorings to watch her sink, one of the dock deputies chased them away."
"Right" said Martin as we pulled alongside.
"I'll get dressed and go down and have a look for her."

Martin began by searching alongside the quay wall itself, but found nothing. He then began swinging out on a search line and again found nothing on his first two sweeps. Halfway through his third sweep we saw his half circle break it's uniform curve.
"You are around something now Martin" George said.
"Yes George I felt that, I am travelling in on the search line now," moments later he said,
"Ok it's the Yo-Yo alright, sitting upright on the bottom, put Bobby on the 'phone George." Standing beside George at the 'phone I depressed the speak switch,
"Go ahead Martin" I said.
"Bobby, how far am I off the quayside here, can the crane reach over to me?"
"Yes Martin, no problem, he'll be less than forty five degrees of an angle, he can reach you comfortably."
"OK Bobby send the crane down."

I gave Willie a shout on the quayside,
"Right Bill, he's beside the boat, jib down over his bubbles and drop the spreader bars down to him." Willie began to jib out until his hook hung above Martin's bubbles and began lowering away slowly. After a few minutes Martin called,
"OK hold that" and we waited patiently until he had the belly lines slung under the launch. Then Martin said,

"Take up my lines and take me away." Andrew quoted his customary answer to that, through clenched teeth.

"Aye they want to take you away. you big bent nosed German bastard." Martin came up onto the ladder and George removed his weights and helmet.

He turned to look at Willie in the crane, "OK" he called over to him,

"take her up nice and steady Billy."

When the boat reached the surface and her gunnel just came out of the water I called out loudly,

"Hold it Bill"

Martin turned towards me and said angrily,

"I'm diving, he does what I tell him to do, not you" then he turned again to Willie and called loudly,

"Take her up and away Willie." I could not believe he was calling for the launch to be lifted out full to the gunnels with water.

We always stopped any sunken craft as soon as their gunnels were inches above the surface, then bailed, or pumped them out. We would never consider hauling any craft out carrying many tons of water inside them. The Yo-Yo was a large launch which had a small cabin up forward and a powerful heavy engine amidships. No timber ship of her size could withstand such a colossal weight of water inside her and as soon as the crane lifted her clear of the surface the belly wires crushed into her sides and we could hear the cracking and splintering of her timbers and frames before she burst open like an egg being dropped on to a concrete floor and emptied out all the weight of water which had completely destroyed her.

The crane driver swung the shattered remains of the Yo-Yo on to the quayside, as Arthur Peebles started walking away calling back sarcastically to Martin.
"Thanks very much Martin for nothing at all."
As Martin sat down on the dressing stool to have his gear removed he said
"I don't know why he got so annoyed, anybody could see his boat was old and rotten to the core." George knelt down to take off Martin's boots just as Jimmy came in to the cabin saying,

"What a bastard, that's a hundred quids worth gone down the drain, I have just lost my hearing aid over the side."
Martin stopped George from removing his boots and asked
"Do you know the exact spot it fell in.?"
"Yes" Jimmy said pointing out of the port hole,
"right under that quayside mooring bollard."
"Are you sure of that?" Martin asked.
"Aye, I tried to grab it but it sank too fast."
"Right" said Martin,
"start up the compressor again and get me dressed and I will get it back for you."

He had the lads move the boat along the quayside until the diving ladder was immediately under the bollard Jimmy had pointed at. Standing back on the ladder, Martin stopped George from dropping the shot weight back over the side.
"No shot line George" he said.
"now listen, I will tell you what I want you to do, I want you to lower me slowly down to twenty-five feet deep and stop me there, then when I say Right, lower me slowly on down but be prepared to pull me back upwards at real speed when I give you a shout, got that George."

"Right Martin, I've got that," George agreed.

I was curious as I tried to work out what Martin was trying to do. Jimmy's hearing aid was about one and a half inches long and three quarters of an inch wide by half an inch, it was tiny and I felt Martin did not have one chance in a thousand of finding it on a thick silt bottom such as was under us at that moment.

George put Martin's helmet on and with the front light screwed in place, Martin called for his air intake to be slightly reduced then slipped off the ladder. George began lowering Martin by hand while I called his depth, reading it from the gauges and George stopped him as I reported.

"Right Martin all held at twenty-five feet deep." After a few moments of silence Martin sounded excited as he said

"Right George lower away," and George dropped him slowly and steadily. In a much louder voice Martin called,

"Take me up quickly, TAKE ME UP." he shouted aloud.

George hauled away at Martin's lines and Martin exploded out of the water almost as high as his waist belt before dropping back to the level of his corselet. In his bare right hand Martin held Jimmy's hearing aid.

I could hardly believe this, he had found it, and yet I knew as soon as our boots touched the bottom we were rendered completely blind by the cloud that always boiled up from the silt instantaneously.

Jonathan had remained sitting down comfortably on the roof of the cabin and had watched the whole sad affair with the Yo-Yo, as if really interested in what was going on and when we set off sailing back to our berth, the bird stood up and offered his outstretched wings to the breeze we were heading into. He made no attempt to fly, but continually altered the angle of his wings, which had the effect of almost lifting him off the roof of the cabin one minute and then forcing him down into a sitting position the next. He continued with this form of exercise all the way back to our berth and I had the feeling it would not be very long before the call of the wild would take him away from me for ever.

As we turned into the basin to come alongside. Jonathan took off from the cabin top. He flew low over the surface of the water with his bare bottom hanging down behind him until it struck the water and he nose dived below the surface. We made fast to the quayside and watched a most indignant bird paddling along towards us. He allowed me to lift him aboard and then walked right through to the compressor room and climbed in his box and with his funny looking bare bottom wiggling from side to side, he snuggled down inside the woollens and in doing so, made it plain he had no intention of leaving us just yet.

Martin left the boat to walk back to the diving hut as usual, and Andrew said
"Did you see how smug he looked when he came on board? just because he managed to find Jimmy's hearing aid, the old German arrogance came over him right away." George took a mouthful of his coffee and leaned back on the bench seating
"He has phenomenal luck, you must admit" he said.
"I don't know about luck," I remarked,
"that was pretty amazing, recovering something as small as that and I would like to know how he managed it."

Jimmy had opened up his hearing aid and dried it out thoroughly and put it back together again and clipping it behind his ear, he grinned at us saying. "Good old Martin, it's working fine."

"The Boatmen won't be calling him good old Martin after destroying a perfectly good boat," said George.

Andrew handed me a mug of coffee saying,

"You tried to stop him, but he is so thick in the head he would not listen, you knew that was going to happen so why did you not stick to your guns? Willie would have stopped heaving up for you."

"I could not stop him, the man that's diving is in charge and as long as life or limb are not in danger, I don't have the right to stop him." Jimmy passed a plate of biscuits around,

"He can be kind sometimes," he said,

"he did not need to dive again and get my hearing aid back."

"Big deal" said Andrew scornfully, "Ok. he saved you a hundred pounds but he probably cost the Boatmen thousands by his ignorance."

Back in the diving hut I completed my write up of our daily diving diary while Martin sat reading his newspaper.

"Martin" I said,

"how did you manage to find the hearing aid so quickly?"

He folded up his newspaper and smiled at me.

"It's a wee trick I learned years ago, but everything has to be done quickly. When you hung me off at twenty-five feet deep. I pulled myself back up a bit on my own lines and turned completely upside down and had George lower me head first to the bottom, so I did not touch the silt at all and there it was lying ready for me to pick up on top of the silt."

"So that's why you reduced your air intake before you went down, to slow down the speed your legs would inflate while you were upside down."

"Yes and that is why George had to haul me up real fast to get my helmet above the level of my boots otherwise I would have come up feet first and out of control."

"God Martin" I said "I would never have thought of that in a thousand years, especially after reading about so many standard suit men who perished in the past through turning upside down and drowning while wearing leaking suits."

"Yes you have to know what you are doing and do it real quick to get away with it," Martin said proudly.

Chapter 21

The Yellow Valve

"I think he did it deliberately" said Martin, grinning at me, "after all he sat there watching us cleaning the whole boat since we came on board, yet he waited until we were completely finished before he did it."
"I believe you could be right," I agreed,
"there is something about the smug look he gave us, as soon as he did it, as much as to say,
'That's the way I like it finished off.'

It was 7-30 a.m. on a Monday morning and Martin and I had hosed down and cleaned up the amazing amount of the weekend's bird droppings and dried the cabin as much as possible. We were now sitting on a canvas sheet spread over the damp Port side bench seating. Jonathan had watched the whole operation from the opposite side of the boat and had then shown his contempt of our efforts by ejecting a milky white stream over the clean seating. I had mopped it up, while Jonathan appeared to give me an evil looking grin and a quick knowing wink, as if mocking my efforts.

Martin and I then sat back and looked at him. His body plumage was beautiful, fully grown back to its original size and preened to perfection. The shining white smoothness of his feathers abruptly gave way to the contrasting rich colour of sea grey across his back and wings. The overall statement declared a young adult male Herring gull, well fed and in tip top condition. He looked magnificent, even his bottom was now decently clad in half grown tail feathers.

Over the last three weeks I had become aware of the fact he was still growing and I realised he must have been very young when I first found him lying at death's door on the east breakwater. At that time I had taken him for a much older bird, for there had been no sign of the mottled brown feathers of a juvenile. I now knew he must have moulted just before I found him fighting for his very life.

Now he stood with his head almost up to the level of my knees and the once emaciated body had been transformed into a robustness that would have to be seen to be believed.
"When are you going to let him go?" Martin asked.
"Whenever he decides Martin, it is up to him, I will not try to stop him when he does go, but watch this," I said as I took a plateful of small sprats out of my locker and stepped out on to the stern of the boat and tossed them up on the quayside. All the herring gulls sitting on the ridge of Dad's gear shed took to the air instantly and made a dive for the fish.

With a howl of protest Jonathan came thundering out of the cabin and with his bottom still only half supported by the immature tail feathers, he deliberately crash landed on the quayside among the squawking gulls fighting over the sprats, and began pecking at them viciously. The birds scattered in all directions away from him and tried sneaking around him to get back at the fish, while he alternated between swallowing sprats as quickly as he could and snapping and biting at any bird within reach.

After the sprats were all gone, the gulls returned to the shed's ridge and Jonathan stood on the quayside alone. He glared up at the rest of them, then threw back his head and gave voice to a strident challenge, but finding he had no takers, he set off in a lumbering run along the quay and with difficulty took to the air, like an overloaded aircraft. He gained height by wheeling around in tight circles until he was well above the birds on the shed's ridge.

His low slung bottom hung down like the undercarriage of an aeroplane and he suddenly swooped down and deliberately dived into the gulls on the ridge, knocking them over like nine pins.

"He is one hell of a fighter," Martin remarked admiringly and I felt really proud of my boy.

"Yes he certainly gets annoyed if I feed anyone other than him but watch what he does now."

Jonathan stood on the ridge by himself and once more gave voice to a challenge, but no one wanted to know. He was too big and much too rough for all of them. He quit the noisy squawking and looked all around him, squinting one eyed upwards as if checking no would be challenger was trying to catch him unprepared and apparently satisfied there was no enemy around, he fixed his eyes on the two of us in the boat below him.

He stretched his wings out, like a glider and ran down the slates towards the shed's eaves and his trailing tail end appeared to clear the gutter at the bottom with hardly anything at all to spare. He flew over our heads and around the Basin, before coming in lengthwise along the quay and tried to make a landing alongside our boat but his hanging bottom touched down first and with wings still outstretched he pitched forward on his face. He rose back up on his feet in a haughty manner and folded his wings and glared at the two of us, as if he was disgusted at our laughing at his abortive attempt at a graceful touch down.

"Well there is one thing you need never worry about Bobby." Martin said as we watched the bird hop from the quay on to the top of the boat's cabin.
"when he does leave you, he will be able to look after himself for I never saw a bird with such a terrible temper."
"Right enough Martin," I agreed as we climbed ashore and headed for David Grieve's office.
"the rest of the gulls got out of his way as if it was Jonathan the Terrible coming at them."

"Victoria Dock new timber piles with the Carpenters today Davy" said Martin.
"Oh! NO you are NOT" David exploded loudly, pushing his chair back from his desk and before he could say another word Martin rushed in with.
"Oh! so is it hate the divers week again Davy?" The Works Manager giggled nervously,
"No no Martin Heh! Heh! Heh! its not eh! Its not hate the divers week" said David in an instantly apologetic manner.
"You have to go help an American ship eh! go help an American ship that's in eh! that's in trouble."
"Right David we will go help the American ship that's in trouble." Martin repeated quietly, before asking
"Where exactly is it Davy?"

David's brows came down instantly and he jumped up on his feet and tossed his pen down angrily on his desk top, I remember thinking he might just as well have thrown the pen in his waste paper basket, for he never seemed able to persuade it to write anything, as far as I could see.

"How the bloody hell would I know where it is, go and see eh! go and see the Dockhead or eh! The Harbourmaster or anybody eh! anybody at all that knows about the shipping side of things."
"Ok David" Martin agreed with him,
"we will go see the Dockhead or the Harbour Master or anybody at all that knows anything about the shipping side of things." I could not make up my mind whether Martin was trying to make a fool out of David or not, but whenever this type of charade erupted between the two of them, I felt the whole performance could have stood shoulder to shoulder with the very best of the Christmas Pantomime shows.

"It's not a ship" said Captain Alan Childs, the deputy Harbour Master on duty that day.
"it's one of the American Pipe Slingers." I noticed a glazed look come over Martin's eyes,
"What is a Pipe Slinger Captain?" he asked. The Captain gave a good natured laugh, Alan Childs was the youngest of the Deputy Harbour Masters, he was a very tall man with broad shoulders which were accentuated by an ultra slim waistline, which was unusual among Captains, as most of them seemed to eventually develop a bit of a paunch. He was fair complexioned with blonde wavy hair that had the faintest coppery tinge of red running through it.

"It is a very long floating platform of a craft which the Americans use to weld sections of the oil pipes together on, then one end of it can submerge to a fair old depth to allow divers to lay the pipes as a continuous pipeline along the seabed," the Captain explained, before pointing out of his office windows.

"Anyway Martin, you better get cracking because it has been called as an emergency and here comes the Oxcar towing your barge to take you out to her."

"Ok Captain" Martin said as we turned to leave the Harbour Office,

"we will get on board and thank you for now."

Martin's manners were impeccable, although at times they bordered on the obsequious, when dealing with all of the senior staff of the Leith Docks Commission, the only exception being our own Works Manager.

On board our Barge, Martin began dressing in his woollens as the Oxcar towed us out into the Forth estuary to meet up with the Pipe Slinger. The weather was fine with hardly a breath of wind and the surface of the sea rippled with small wavelets that shimmered in the morning sunshine. We could not have had better diving conditions as we came alongside the extraordinarily long platformed craft.

The first thing we noticed was the tremendous roar of two huge compressors, one mounted on the port side and the other on the starboard side of her upper deck housing and both of them going full bore. An American seaman caught our mooring ropes and secured them around the Slingers bollards. "Oh! Oh!" he said,

"here comes the skipper."

A very fat man was waddling along the deck of the Slinger towards us. He wore an outsize blue boiler suit which his body more than filled to capacity and with the sleeves rolled up over his elbows, his podgy small looking arms swung back and forth rapidly in his haste to reach us. His black, wavy, Italian looking hair straggled down over a sweat drenched, agitated face. He stepped on board our barge and entered the cabin where Martin sat almost fully dressed except for weights and helmet. The skipper's bulbous fat lips hung open as his breath rasped in and out of them.

"Diver" he panted,
"one of ma Gawd damned men has left the by pass valve wide open with the tanks vent valve shut, so we are going to go down if you can't help us. We can no longer reach the manifold ourselves, it is far too deeply submerged and our compressors won't keep us afloat for much longer." I watched the glazed look return to Martin's face as he tried to follow the skipper's rapid fire outburst.

"We need to drop you down on to the manifold and when you get there you must close the blue by pass valve and open the brown vent valve, but whatever you do, don't touch the yella valve, it must stay closed." The bemused look remained on Martin's face and I was pretty sure he had not grasped what was required of him, but he did not ask any questions of the Skipper, as George finished lashing his boots around his ankles.

The American sailor appeared rowing a small dinghy and came alongside our barge. He was obviously used with working with Divers as he said.

"If you give me your shot weight, I will row out and drop it down alongside of our air manifold." Andrew loaded our shot weight aboard his boat and he rowed away with it over open water until he came to an eruption of air blowing on the surface. He stopped the dinghy close to the blow of air and lowered our shot weight over the side of his boat and I then realised the Slinger must be a much longer craft than I first thought, because he was a fair old distance away from us. He dropped the slack over the side and I made the free end of the shot line fast to the diving ladder as George prepared to pass the helmet over Martin's head, but before he could do so the agitated skipper laid one podgy hand on Martin's shoulder and stared wildly into the diver's eyes, as all the pent up emotion of possibly losing his craft caused him to entreat Martin to save it. The words flew from the fat lips like machine gun bullets.

"Don't touch the yella valve diver, just close the blue valve and open the brown one. Don't touch the yella valve, the yella valve has 128 p.s.i on it, so for Gawd's sake don't touch the yella valve, whatever you do." He stepped back on board his own craft and walked away a short distance, then turned and stood watching us anxiously.

George put the helmet on Martin and down he went. We watched his bubbles progress over the open water and then stop fairly close to the existing blow of air on the surface. Not one word came over the diver phone as the minutes ticked away. After some time, I thought to myself,'Come on Martin,' for I was watching the water level rising as it advanced, creeping slowly up the inclined deck of the Slinger. George whispered quietly

"He is worried about something again," he was being careful the skipper could not hear him. Andrew cupped one hand to shield his mouth on the skipper's side,
"I think the Yank gave him too many instructions" he whispered sarcastically,
"after all, he was told to close a blue valve and open a brown one, does the Yank think Martin can work out all that lot by himself."

The skipper came hurrying back along his deck towards us.
"What is he doing now?" he asked, in a harassed exasperated voice, wiping the sweat off his forehead with the palm of one hand. George depressed the speak switch,
"The skipper wants to know what you are doing now Martin?"
"Aw! Hold on for a bloody minute" Martin shouted angrily.
The skipper shook his head at the diver's angry retort and walked away from us again, remarking gloomily as he did so,
"We don't have too many minutes left before we will have to abandon her, for the compressors are fighting a losing battle."

I looked up at the blue haze of smoke coming from both of the compressors and I knew the American Skipper was right, the Rolls Royce engines were running flat out, and at the moment they were proving a testimony to the workmanship of the engineering Company that had built them, but I wondered how long they could take such continual punishment before exploding. The blow of air on the surface from an open valve obviously meant they were continually trying to compress fresh air into fresh air endlessly.

We were all standing silently waiting for a response from Martin but not one word came over the phone.

"I wonder what the hell he is doing," I said quietly. Andrew gave his usual dry laugh,

"He will be wondering what the hell he is doing as well." he said.

A sudden wild and violent hissing noise came up over the diver phone and seconds later the surface erupted with a tremendous blow of air.

"Oh! My Gawd" exclaimed the skipper in horror,

"he has opened the yella valve with the blue by pass still wide open as well." While the skipper was talking Martin appeared on the surface lying flat out, obviously blown to the surface by the force of the highly compressed air. George and Andrew began hurriedly hauling in the slack of his lines to make contact with the out of control diver and then began towing him towards our barge. I immediately noticed the water level was no longer creeping along the Slinger's deck for now it was advancing quite quickly.

"Take your diver up and bring him on board," the skipper ordered in a loud commanding voice,

"that's it, we have to abandon her now and get clear before she goes down,"

Martin had not uttered one word while this was all happening but when George told him the skipper had ordered us to bring him on board immediately he exploded.

"Never mind the bloody skipper," he roared over the phone, "give me slack, I am going back down to fix it." The lads looked at me and I shrugged my shoulders as Martin gripped the shot line and slipped off the ladder once more.

I looked at the far end of the floating part of the Slinger and watched it slowly start to inch upwards. It would soon be out of the water altogether. With more than half of the overall length submerged it was now cantilevering the floating remainder up out of the sea. The skipper warned us she would go suddenly in the end and advised us it was not just our diver who was at risk and we should take him on board and pull away clear, as quickly as we could

All my life I have never been a man prone to panic in an emergency but now my brain was racing along, as I heard the American Skipper call across to the Oxcar to tow us clear, as soon as we had Martin aboard. We could no longer distinguish his surface bubbles for they were lost in the colossal blow of air all around and Martin had not uttered another word over the phone. I depressed the speak switch.

"Martin come up right now or we will haul you up." I ordered.

"WILL YOU HANG ON FOR A COUPLE OF MINUTES." Martin screamed hysterically.

I was reluctant to have the lads heave on his lines for fear we might foul them around the manifold or any other obstruction that might be down there, but by now I was in a right quandary.

"If the 'phone should go on the blink," I said to George and Andrew, trying hard to think of whatever else could possibly go wrong.

"Give him a quick hand signal to come up and if he does not answer it immediately, then we will have to drag him up bodily."

"The yanks are leaving," said George, pointing to the Slinger's motor launch pulling away with the Skipper and his crew men on board.

"Martin" I said much more forcefully over the phone, "COME UP, NOW."

The furthest floating end of the craft was now clear of the surface and rising steadily higher into the air as I watched it. The roar of the compressors changed their tone as they began listing towards the sunken end of the craft

"FOR FUCK'S SAKE," Martin yelled, "I AM ALMOST THERE GIVE ME TWO MORE MINUTES."

I felt we had no more time left to give him and I moved away from the phone and towards the lads to help them drag the diver to the surface forcibly, against his will, and possibly save his life, when the big blow of air abruptly stopped. The sudden silence instead of the wildly hissing air halted me before I reached the lads and I also realised the roar of the two compressors was easing down considerably and they now began to sound as if they were pumping against a back pressure, instead of fresh air.

Against all the odds, Martin must have managed some how to get under that monumental force of escaping pressurised air and turned it off. He had also obviously closed down the blue valve and opened up the brown one, for in a very short time we watched the invading sea stop its relentless advancement and seemingly begin to reluctantly recede, as slowly as an ebbing tide. The far floating end began once more lowering itself back into the water and the compressors mournful song changed back down into a slower deep throated roar. They had been working so hard the whole time, that I would not have been surprised if they had both burst into flames at any moment.

"Take up my lines," said Martin,

"I am going to spindle up, take me away." The lads brought him across the surface towards the diving ladder as Andrew once more remarked. "If they would only take you away, you thick headed bastard, this job could be so good."

Standing on the ladder, with helmet and weights removed, Martin looked round at the Slinger.

"God!" he exclaimed,

"that's some bloody list she has, it's a wonder she can still float at an angle like that." By some strange means Martin appeared unable to grasp the fact that he alone was responsible for the near loss of the craft, because of the stupid mistake he had made.

The Americans came back on board and the Skipper sent one man up on to the Deck housing to ease the compressors down to their normal working speed. We stayed alongside until the manifold ebbed up clear of the sea altogether and I was astonished at the overall length of the working platform of the craft, now that I could see it all, floating on an even keel. When we arrived back at our own berth, the condemnation of Martin began as soon as he left the Barge to go up to the diving hut.

"He might have managed all right if the Yank had never mentioned the yellow valve in the first place," George said,

"How do you make that out?" asked Andrew,

"after all the Yank told him to his face not to touch it."

George swung his feet up on the seat and stretched out with his back against the compressor room bulkhead.

"I know, but he gets confused easily," he said,

"and if the Yank had only said close the blue one and open the brown one, he could not possibly get that wrong."

"I would not bet on it," said Andrew handing me a cup of coffee, "he is so thick in the head he might just have made the right choice but even that would have been by pure luck on a fifty-fifty chance."

Our boatman, wee Jimmy Robertson passed out a plate of biscuits.

"If there is a wrong way of doing something," he said, "Martin Bendicks will find it, but he once did something right first time."

"Pray tell me Jimmy, when was that, because I could not have been on board at the time," said Andrew.

"Aye but you were there Andrew, I'm talking about the time he picked my hearing aid up off the bottom when I dropped it over the side."

"Oh! yes I remember that, but was that not the same day he showed everybody just how stupid and arrogant he was by destroying the Boatmen's launch the YO-YO."

I had to leave the boat to go up to the diving hut to fill in my daily diving diary so I left them tearing Martin's character to pieces, like a pack of hungry wolves savaging the corpse of their kill. When I walked in the diving hut Martin was sitting reading his newspaper and I sat down at the table and opened up my diary. We sat there in silence as I wrote up the diary, then Martin folded up his paper and said,

"Can I ask you a question Bobby?"

"Certainly Martin, hurl it at me" I said laying aside the diary.

"What did that Yank mean when he said the yellow valve had 128 pee ess eye on it."

I could not believe what I was hearing, this was a diver with almost a quarter of a century's experience behind him, asking the most elemental of all diving questions. A man who could at times come out with some great ideas of how to go about certain underwater jobs, and at other times make such crass stupid mistakes that boggled my mind completely. Wearing an impassive look on my face to hide the shock of such a question I said.

"He meant the yellow valve was connected to his main high pressure storage holding tanks and had a pressure of 128 pounds to the square inch on them Martin, and I honestly will never know how in hell's name you ever managed to get it turned off." Martin smiled at me as if I was actually praising him and he began smirking with pleasure as he said.

"I lay flat out on the deck and crawled under it and tied my belly safety line to the base of a stanchion so it could not blow me back to the surface again. Then I reached up to shut it off, but my God it was hard and it felt like it was trying to tear both my arms off."

I listened to him in utter astonishment and once more I felt that involuntary shudder of horror pass through my body. In the most matter of fact way, he was telling me he had *tied himself to a stanchion*. He had actually lashed himself to the sinking craft and we would not have been able to drag him to the surface if she had gone down at that moment.

Our 56 ton Diving Barge would have resisted the Slinger's attempt to drag us down with her, at least until Martin's safety line snapped. This meant his safety line would have cut him clean in half before reaching its breaking strain and all because he had *"Lashed himself to a stanchion."*

Chapter 22

The Deep water Buoy

It was 7 o'clock on a bitter cold winter's night when the call out came from the Harbour Master's Office. The message simply said I had to report for work immediately. I had been at home for less than two hours and I was not particularly enamoured at the prospect of diving again that night, for that morning my lines men George and Andrew had to use a 56 pound weight to smash up 3 inches of thick ice on the surface to let me enter the water, to work on the Imperial Dry Dock sluice Paddle.

  I had been forced to work with bare hands in order to feel and thread the new bolts I fitted on the Paddle's hydraulic arm, which raises or lowers it when in use, and when I spindled up carefully, after completing the job, my helmet bumped up against the underside of the thick ice and scraped along its entire length as the lads towed me back to the hole that had allowed me to go down in the first place. I then climbed out and stood on the diving ladder and after the lads had taken off my weights and helmet, I cupped my frozen hands, while Mother Nature drove small pins into the quick of the flesh under my finger nails and continued the agony until the circulation returned.

Arriving back at the Docks, I found I was the last man to turn out. The steam Tug Craigleith had broken up all the thick ice in the Basin that surrounded the Digger and our diving barge. Bunty, the skipper of the Digger and his crew were already on board and I could also see the bogey fire on our Barge was glowing red in the darkness and its cheery brightness helped dispel some of the miserable feeling I was experiencing, brought on by the cold dreariness of that wintry night. The diving team were aboard our Barge and I could see they were busily securing it alongside the digger, so the tug could take both of us in tow together.

"What's the job?" I asked jumping aboard our Barge.
"The deep water marker buoy that lies off Inchkeith Island has disappeared." said Andrew.
"The Harbour Master thinks it may have been hit and holed by a ship and has sunk at it's mooring. He wants us to go out and recover it." said George.

We set off, with the Craigleith shouldering the ice aside on our way out the Fairway towards the open sea. We had the Shetlander Arthur Robertson with us, as a spare hand aboard our Barge. As an ex sailor, Arthur could turn his hand to just about anything relating to seafaring. The tug sailed past the brightly lit up cellular Dam around the construction work of the new Locks and out into the misty black dark of the Firth of Forth and shortly after that, she positioned us over the approximate area the Buoy normally occupied and the lads dressed me to make the dive.

Standing on the diving ladder and almost ready to go, I looked up at the swirling sleet and snow descending out of the inky blackness of the night. The snow flakes were large and soft as lambs fleece as they landed on my face and instantly melted but the sleet was small, rounded and extremely hard and stung the skin with an impact like small grains of ice cold sand particles.

There was something comforting about the bright lights of the Digger and the loud thrum of the Tug's engines, which should alert any merchant ship in the vicinity.

George lifted my helmet over my head and once more I was inside a much smaller world. If anything the thrum of the Tug's engines, coupled with the deisel knock-knocking of our own compressor, intensified the sounds by funnelling them through the open front of my helmet.

George screwed in my front light and instantly all outside noise fell silent and the only sound came from the hiss of my incoming air. As usual the sudden restriction of all of the outside sound to my ears was accompanied by a heightening of my sense of smell and I was conscious once again of the damp rubbery odour of my incoming air.

"Phone o.k." came Andrew's voice from the speaker in the top of my helmet.

"Fine Andrew" I replied as George handed me the shot line and slapped the top of my helmet. I slipped into the freezing surface water and began dropping quite fast. Every now and then I stopped my descent by hanging onto the shot line for a short while, to allow the diving pump to catch up with the increasing pressure. As I carried on downwards I was surrounded by a pitch blackness which was surreal in it's quietude and tranquillity. Below me, my torch, mounted on a bracket on the side of my helmet, cast its beam downwards and picked out the misty approach of the sea bed.

"On the bottom" I said as I landed on an uneven sea bed and stumbled over a small boulder.

"You are on the bottom" George answered. My torch allowed me to see about ten feet in front of me before it's light was curtailed by the vastness of the dark water surrounding me.

"No sign of the mooring chains anywhere around me at the moment, can you get the tug skipper to give me a search direction."

Martin came on the phone. "I think we should be a bit nearer Inchkeith Island as I remember, but hang fire until we find out what the Skipper says."

"Hanging fire it is" I replied as I leaned against a barnacle encrusted boulder. The bottom was strewn with loose small to medium sized rocks covered in carpets of sea weed and lying on ledges of steeply inclined solid rock which always tore at our suits as we moved across it. The sharp marine growth of mussels, limpets and barnacles clinging to every rock face abraded the knees and elbows of our suits so much, that we often sprung small leaks, which were most uncomfortable in the freezing winter water. Even our rubber gloves were very quickly abraded as we hauled ourselves over such a nightmare of a sea bed.

Very often we would return to the surface after searching across an area such as this to find the skin of our hands had also been rubbed raw and were bleeding in places.

"Ok Bobby" George said.

"set off, so I see which way you are facing." I began slowly clambering over the uneven bottom and silently cursing my Bosses who refused to let me use my Avon dry suit and flippers. The skin suit was ideal for both this kind of sea bed and also for examining a ship's bottom in mid water but I was told the Commission's insurance only covered Standard Hard Hat gear.

"Turn around and head off in the opposite direction," said George.

"Right George," I answered and headed back the way I had just come. Slithering and sliding over the inclined ledges of rock I was relieved to come across a flattish area of sand and began to make good progress. Now down on all fours I was travelling quite quickly.

Suddenly I stopped and felt the hair rise at the nape of my neck. Some considerable distance away from me and high above the sea bed, I could see a small electric blue light flashing intermittently out of the darkness. To me it instantly conveyed a feeling of menace, as it appeared to take the shape of a small Alien space craft hovering in the mid water, and I stayed still for some minutes watching it, while my brain wrestled between fantasy and logic.

Strange what tricks the human brain can play on us when we come across something we cannot immediately rationalise. I found I had automatically stuffed both hands behind my front lead weight in some kind of reflex reaction to imminent danger, but of course this is only useful when being threatened or attacked by Moray eels or Porbeagle sharks. A feeling of helplessness was winning over logic as I considered I was alone on the sea bed and apparently being observed by creatures from outer space. The eerie feeling still stayed with me as the logic began to slowly take over. It must be the Basket Buoy, I thought, it HAS to be the Buoy but then again the Buoy should have a flashing green light not electric blue. and how could it's light still be functioning in deep water? The Buoy itself was about 8 feet high but I was looking at a light much higher above the bottom than that and the Buoy being built of all metal should sink right to the bottom. Could it have landed on a high ledge of rock?

"You have been in one place for some time," said George "have you found it, or is there something bothering you?"

"I think I have found it George, and yes something is bothering me at the moment." I answered as I moved cautiously forward once more, then the large links of a mooring chain came into the beam of my torch. They were lying along the bottom and leading straight towards the flashing light. With an overwhelming feeling of relief I began moving forward confidently once more.

"Yes I am heading towards it now George"

I approached with a return of caution for the flashing light was away high above the seabed and as I came nearer, I watched it slowly changing colour from electric blue to a paler bluey green and as I came closer still, the colour began changing steadily towards a bright green light. I never fail to be amazed at the sea's underwater ability to change all the colours of the spectrum in a never ending display of its versatility, altering hues of colour as certain conditions undergo a change.

Another twenty yards and there she was, resting solidly on a high ledge of rock rising above the sand.

"Ok George I am right beside it, bring the Digger's crane over my bubbles."

Some time later with the Buoy safely on the deck of the Digger and with my decompression almost complete, George hauled me up to my last stop at ten feet below the boat and I asked. "How long have I got here George?"

"You have another 75 minutes before coming on board"

"Did you say the Buoy's light is still flashing on the deck of the Digger, George?" I asked

"Yes the Tug Skipper said the battery is inside a watertight box capable of withstanding 10 atmospheres of pressure. He also said the Harbour Master was right and the Buoy has been holed by a ship, so it will have to be repaired before being put back."

I hung there for a while, exercising energetically with both arms and legs to expel nitrogen from my body and also to promote a bit of heat. I did not have to hold on to the shot line while doing this as George hauled me up to each successive level then tied me off using a series of figure of eight turns of my lines around the stringers of the diving ladder. After a while I again asked,

"How long have I got to go now George?"

"You still have 45 minutes left"

"How is the time, will we manage a couple of pints when we get back in to Leith?"

"I don't think so" George answered. I thought for a few minutes then said.

"Just take me aboard now George and we will manage a pint or two before we go home."

"No" George answered

"What do you mean NO?" I asked aggressively

"I mean NO," said George defiantly,

"I was taught to give my diver everything he wants except death." I had no answer to that.

"Ok George you are right and I am wrong for asking in the first place." I had to admit I was wrong because I had quoted the old adage so many times in the past, in front of linesmen, and cutting decompression times is most definitely dangerous.

We had a trouble free run back to the harbour after I surfaced, and with everything secured we found we had time to spare and could manage a few pints before going home after all. Our Boatman, wee Jimmy was the only man to set off on his way home but the rest of the team along with our spare hand Arthur Robertson settled ourselves in Charlie's Bar and I called the first round of "Five pints Charlie, if you please." We settled in a very convivial atmosphere aided by more beer as Martin, George and Andrew each stood a round over the next hour.

At six minutes to 10 o'clock the first bell began it's continuous clamour before stopping one minute later, warning all patrons they had only five minutes left in which to order from the bar. Big Arthur was telling stories about his childhood on a croft on the island of Yell in the Shetland Isles. He appeared to be particularly animated as he described some of the things he had endured as a young boy.

"My faither had ordered two young Clydesdale horses to be ferried up from Aberdeen on the Saint Clair, to work on wir croft. They were landed at Lerwick and transferred to the Earl of Zetland to be brought up to Yell. Faither sent me to Lerwick to take charge of them and come back to Yell wi' them. We hed to lay off from the island when we got there, for the Earl hed no harbour to go in to, in those days. The horses were too big and too heavy to be carried ashore in the Flitt boat, which landed all the islands provisions for a week, but efter the Earl anchored off shore, they pit a belly band under the young horses, wan at a time and lifted them ower the side of the ship. I was only twelve years of age at the time but with me sitting on the first ane, I steered him towards the shore and the ither ane followed us as we swam to the beach."

The words flew from Arthur's mouth faster and faster, then louder and louder as he tried to speak over the top of the noise of the last bell, at one minute to 10 o'clock. The bell stopped, and so did Arthur. He looked up apparently mystified saying,
"That wisna the last bell wis it?"
"Yes, that was the last bell," said Andrew sarcastically, because Arthur had been given the name of a bit of a tight wad and it was said he would try anything to avoid paying for a drink.
"Damn it," said Arthur.
"I wis jist goin' tae order up drams and pints a'roond."
He must have felt he was pretty safe at that time, for most Publicans obeyed the law and refused to serve another drink after the last bell.
"What was that you said Arthur?" Andrew asked loudly.
"Man" Arthur replied, in a disappointed tone of voice.
"I wis jist aboot tae order drams and pints for everybody, I did not realise that wis the last bell."
"CHARLIE" Andrew bellowed, "ARTHUR HERE WANTS DRAMS AND PINTS FOR EVERYBODY."
"But,but" Arthur stammered,
"I thought you said yon was the last bell,"
"Coming right up lads," said Charlie. It seemed he did not give a damn for the law and often served more Policemen after hours than anybody else.

Arthur tried his best to hide his feelings as he slowly and reluctantly withdrew the notes from his wallet, while with a smile on their faces both George and Andrew raised their dram glasses on high and said in unison, "Cheers Arthur."

Chapter 23

The Old Dock

Martin and I entered David Grieve's office one morning to find our Works Manager standing behind his desk with a very worried look on his face.
"Martin you are eh! working for me, of course, but eh! working for the Harbour Master eh! working for the Harbour Master at the same time." Something had well and truly upset him and the giveaway was the high colour in his cheeks coupled with the highly agitated manner. Whatever the reason, it appeared to have caused his brain to race away ahead of his ability to speak altogether.

"You have to eh! get boats, eh! Some -----boats and burn them. What I mean is, -----we have to eh! we have to clear the old Dock in a hurry, you have to go and see eh! Go and see the Harbour Master eh!" He dried up completely and a wild-eyed look came over his face as he tried to put words together in a lucid form, before finally blustering out loudly.
"Just Go Now and see the Harbour Master."
"Right Dave we will go and see the Harbour Master now," said Martin and we left David's office and walked away towards the Harbour Master's building.

"He is in a bit of a state, I wonder what has happened to get him all worked up like that?" said Martin,
"I have trouble understanding him at the best of times and I found out long ago it calms him down if you just agree with him, even although you don't have a clue what the hell he is talking about." I began laughing and Martin said.
"What's funny about that?"
"I was just thinking, you don't always agree with him, especially when you shout at him "What is this Davy, is it hate the Diver week again."
"Ah! but that is only when he gets me all worked up as well Bobby."

Arriving at the Harbour Master's office, we found Douglas Gray, the Harbour Master was expecting us.
"There is a bit of a panic on, lads" he said, in his American like nasal twang, which had earned him the nickname of 'The Newhaven Yank,' bestowed upon him by the Dock's labour force.
"we have to get the Old Dock clear of all the small cabin cruisers and pleasure yachts that are berthed there. It seems some time ago David Grieve was told to write to the owners of these boats and inform them they must leave the Old Dock by September this year, but Dave only managed to contact about half of the owners and he has just found out those he could not contact are owe the Commission a small fortune in Harbour dues and David cannot trace any of them."
"What happens to their boats now Captain?" I asked

"Dick Godden has ordered them to be towed over to the Tip to the west of Rank's Mill at high tide and there, they are to be burned."

"I have seen some of these boats Captain, and there are some damn good Cabin Cruisers and yachts among them." I said.

"That does not matter Bob" said Douglas,

"no one wants to admit the boats belong to them, because it would cost them far more than the boats are worth, so obviously the owners don't care what happens to them," and he handed Martin a list of the condemned boats.

"You lads and your diving boat are to work with Norman and Arthur aboard the Figgate and that is a list of the names of the boats you are to tow over to the Tip at high water and when the tide ebbs you are to set them on fire and burn them."

"Right Captain burn them it is." said Martin in a somewhat happy voice as we took our leave of the Harbour Master and returned on board our own boat, which had the Figgate moored alongside of it.

Two hours before high water we entered the Old Dock accompanied by the Figgate. Many of the abandoned craft were little more than derelicts, in a sorry state, and we singled them out first and after pumping them dry we towed one each and landed them on the beach Tip, to the west of Rank's Mill and after the tide ebbed and left them high and dry, we put them to the torch.

This caused quite a bit of consternation to the Tip's watchman, who came rushing down the beach demanding to know who we were and what the hell we thought we were doing there. We showed him the letter signed by Mr.

Godden and he calmed down and left us alone after that. Some of the worst of the neglected boats in the Old Dock had sunk alongside their neighbours and we had to dive to retrieve them from the bottom.

We used Bill Kerr's mobile Neals crane to heave them to the surface and I did notice that while he was diving Martin had them stopped just above the surface level and then pumped out until they were floating. I felt it was a pity he had not treated the YO-YO in the same kindly fashion. We worked away systematically through many of the small craft day after day and at the finish we were destroying some really good looking and apparently perfectly serviceable small yachts and Cabin Cruisers.

In the end only two full size old three masted Barques remained moored side by side. They presented their stern gangways to the west cross berth adjacent to the Caledonian Gates and the Railway Station of the same name. One was the SS Dolphin, a merchant naval training ship and the other was H M S Claverhouse a Royal Naval training ship. The latter was equipped with a full sized gymnasium, which had a professional boxing ring erected in it and it was on board this ship I first trained as a boxer with Petty Officer 'Tosh' Main the former Welterweight Champion of the Royal Navy.

After clearing away the last of the small boats we settled down to have our afternoon coffee in the cabin of the diving boat along with Norman and big Arthur. Martin had left the boat and gone off to make his own way back to the diving hut, which he did on a regular basis. Once again the conversation turned to the complex character and oddball behaviour of Martin.

"He looked like he was enjoying burning the boats" George said shaking his head at the sad thought.

"Of course he was," said Andrew,

"the big German bastard just glories in destroying anything. He was probably happy because it was all official, instead of being caused by the stupid mistakes he makes while trying to rescue something or other, like for instance the YO-YO."

"Ah! That wass a most terrible shame," said Norman, again in his quaintly hissing Hebridean accent.

"for she wass a bonny boat."

"She wisna sae bonny efter Martin wis feenished wi' her," said big Arthur, with a laugh.

I left them to their castigation of my diving Buddy and stepped out into the stern cockpit with my coffee. I looked across at HMS Claverhouse and found myself thinking back fondly over my boxing training days aboard her in the late nineteen forties. Both Petty Officer Tosh Main and I had made it through to the semi-finals of the Naval Boxing Championships to be decided in Newcastle in 1951. I fought at light Welterweight and Tosh at Welterweight.

On the morning of my bout in Newcastle, I was accompanied to the weigh in by my ring second Chief Petty Officer Dick Cunningham and Tosh. I stepped on the scales and the Lieutenant-Commander-Surgeon weighed me and declared I was two pounds too heavy.

"You have time to get him to shed the extra weight." he said to C.P.O. Cunningham and Tosh.

"He does not fight until 4-30 pm this afternoon and I can weigh him in at any time up to 2-30 pm if you want to try it"

"Right" said Tosh with a strange look of determination on his face,

"I'll get the weight off him and bring him back again, or kill him in the attempt." He and Dick had a quick whispered confab together and Tosh rushed away while the C.P.O. led me down to the Boiler Room under the Arena. I had no idea what they intended to do to me and I stood there in my bare feet and wearing only my Boxer shorts and wondered what they were about to try. I was not long in finding out for Tosh arrived carrying an armful of seamen's Polar ice jerseys and training skipping ropes. They opened up the furnace doors and soon had me standing in front of the raging fire wearing three of the Polar ice jerseys at once. I was handed the skipping ropes and told to go for it.

In the next half an hour the sweat poured off me as I skipped as if my life depended on it. I was then rubbed down and rushed back up to the weighing room and on to the scales once more. The surgeon adjusted the scales then shook his head.
"Still the same, he is still two pounds over weight."
"Get the boxer shorts off," said Tosh and I shucked them off.
"and the protecter," I gave him a hard look, thinking he was trying to be funny but he meant it, so I took it off and stood back on the scales completely naked. The surgeon tried again and once more shook his head.

"He is a very fit laddie but I am afraid he will be unable to get down to the weight of light Welterweight for much longer because his build suggests he is ready to step up a weight. He is still slightly over," he said. Then staring hard deliberately at my groin he turned and grinned at Tosh and Dick.

"Give me two minutes with my scalpel and I will guarantee he will be well and truly inside the required weight," he said cheekily.

I was once again rushed back down to the boiler room, re-clad in the jerseys and resumed my skipping in front of the open fire. After a while I said,
"Did you know Tosh, the Chinese had a word for this?"
"What was that?" he asked innocently.
"They called it torture" I replied.

I made the weight at my third and final attempt and Tosh, who was a man in his thirties at that time and who was a natural Welterweight, explained that one day I would probably mature into a Cruiserweight or even a Heavyweight. Time did prove him right in the end and this would be the last time I ever fought at light Welterweight.

On the way back to our Hotel I said.
"Tosh at the moment I would not be capable of punching my way out of a paper bag, I am completely exhausted."
"Don't worry about it Laddie we have a few hours before you fight and when we get back to the Hotel you will get a drink of lime juice and some Protein in the form of a small steak and at least two hours sleep or rest."
"Yes" agreed the C.P.O.
"and when you climb in the ring all the weight will be back, you are taller than Leading Seaman Steven Harris, you will be at least four pounds heavier than he is and with a longer reach you will have all the advantages." Tosh nudged me with his elbow as we walked along and winked.
"Poor Steve will find he is really up against a Welterweight." he said. Most of their predictions did in fact

come true but not all of them. By the time I climbed in the ring I felt as strong as a horse and my earlier exhaustion had completely gone.

In the first round Steve and I sparred, as we tried to sound each other out for about the first minute, then I threw a straight right at his chin with all my upper body strength behind it. Steve saw it late and tried to duck under it but he was not quick enough. Instead of his chin I caught him on the right eyebrow and since his head was dropping fast the punch opened a two inch gash across the top of his rather prominent eyebrow. The blood poured down his face and when the bell sounded the end of the first round, I sat on my stool and watched his seconds frantically trying to stem the flow of blood.

I had C.P.O. Cunningham in my corner and he was excited as he said.

"Go for the eye, he can't see you on that side, concentrate on that cut over his eye and you have got him."

Alas I was a fighter and Steve was a boxer and a very good boxer at that. For the rest of the bout I could not get near that damaged eye while Steve's educated left hand did a demolition job on my face. It was demoralising to see the blood pouring down his face and be unable to land another telling blow upon it.

Stevie Harris won a very convincing points victory and sent me home to Edinburgh with a severely bruised face. The Newcastle trip was a disaster for our boxing team, we all lost our semi-finals, except for our Heavyweight, Alex Stevenson, who was lucky enough to go through, by merely entering the ring, there being no opponent to challenge him.

I came out of my daydream of the past when I realised I was hearing the conversation in the boat's cabin behind me. They were still talking about Martin as Norman asked.

"Does he neffer haff a cup of coffee or something to eat here on poard the boat?"

"Never" said George emphatically.

"For a man of his age he hass the most beautiful white teeth." Norman added.

"That's because he never uses them," said Andrew.

"all he eats is a few nuts and raisins and he hardly gets them over his neck before he rushes away to scrub his teeth like mad." Andrew shook his head reproachfully.

"and he would cut your throat for a sixpence, did you know he stole the diving job from Sandy McGill?"

"How did he do that?" big Arthur asked.

"During the war the old Dock Commission diver retired and Sandy's wife Peggy phoned Mr. Godden and made an appointment for Sandy to be interviewed for the job at 5 o'clock that night. Bendicks and Sandy were both working as shipwrights with Menzies ship repairers and Sandy made the mistake of telling Bendicks about his appointment. Bendicks clocked out at dinnertime that day and rushed round to see Mr. Godden and got the job."

"Oh! He surely neffer did that" said an aghast Norman. I turned and looked in to the cabin.

"Oh! Yes Norman" I confirmed,

"I was diving with big Sandy for years and the big man told me that story exactly as Andrew has just told it to you now."

"Oh that wass a terrible thing for him to do" said an obviously horrified Norman.

208

"but when I choined the Commission Sandy wass working with them as a shipwright and he wass very friendly with Martin."

"I don't know why" Andrew said with a look of distaste on his face.

"if he had done that to me I would not have looked at the side of the street he was on ever again. You better watch yourself Bobby for Bendicks could stab you in the back as soon as look at you."

I decided to try and steer the conversation away from the subject of Bendicks so I said.

"I wonder why the Commission are clearing everything out of the Old Dock at this time?"

"Oh!" said Norman, "it iss because they want rid of all the small pleasure craft before the new locks are finished and Leith iss no longer a tidal Port."

"But what difference will that make?" I persisted.

"Well" said Norman, "it iss said they are going to be sharging an awful lot of money to lock shipping in and out of the Port and the wee poat's owners will not be able to afford it, so they want them to transfer to Newhaven or Granton where they can come and go ass they please."

"Right enough," I agreed, "once the New Locks are complete everything, no matter how small, coming or going will have to pass through them.

The Dolphin and Claverhouse have been here in the same position since I was a wee boy so they will not be moving anywhere."

"Well I haff heard that one day they are to be taken out of here ass well, because the Commission are thinking of filling in this Dock and building something or other on top of it," said Norman.

"after all, it's gates and sluices are falling apart and it's wee dry dock iss too small for the shipping of today, so they are going to do away with the lot."

His mention of the little dry dock brought back memories of my first day at work in Henry Robb's shipyard, in the year the war ended. The small graving dock lay directly across the road from the Shipyard's time offices and in my mind's eye I could again see hundreds of men pouring through the time office gates and dropping their little brass discs in the trays lying in front of the time keepers and all to the wail of the all clear air raid siren, now being used to mark the start and the end of each day's work.

I too had raced through these gates and dropped my identification disc numbered 495 with the rest. The rush continued, skirting around the small graving dock and out through the Citadel Gates, where lines of Buses stood awaiting the men. The destination boards on their fronts proclaimed all the various districts around Edinburgh. The ride home was a nightmare in these buses, packed to the gunnels and with men standing all the way. Almost everyone smoked at that time and as soon as they were on board the buses, everyone lit up cigarettes and pipes until the air resembled a blue fog, both upstairs and down.

My day dream began to fade and as it did so, I said to Norman.

"I suppose the Old Dock was built originally for sailing ships and small home trade coasters and with the increased size of shipping today it has had its time and outlived it's usefulness, we should remember, 'All is change or decay."

Chapter 24

Silted Brandy

Martin's bubbles were dribbling up from under the stern of the Roll-on Roll-off ship he was under. He was searching for a weighing machine the Dockers had lost over the side, it was called a steel yard and belonged to the weights and measures department.
"Ok. George I have found it," Martin said over the diver phone,
"It is lying quite close to the quayside and a fair distance under the ship but we can drag it out sideways with the crane before taking it up."
"Got that Martin," George acknowledged,
"soon as the crane arrives I'll lower it as close as I can to the stern of the ship."
"Right George, I'll come back towards you now, so take up my slack." George began retrieving Martin's lines as his diver came back towards him.
    "Hold it George," Martin called loudly. George depressed the speak switch.
"All held Martin" he said, and then there was a prolonged silence. George looked at me as he cocked an ear towards the diver phone, he stayed like that for several minutes.

"He is worried about something or other again" he said. "believe me, he is thinking real hard at the moment." Andrew popped his head out of the cabin.

"He will be trying to remember what he went down there to do," he said whimsically.

We waited some considerable time before Martin spoke again, or rather whispered, in a low voice.

"George put Bobby on the phone." I depressed the speak switch wondering why Martin felt it necessary to whisper so quietly.

"Go ahead Martin" I said in a deliberately much louder voice but his answer was barely audible.

"Is the coast clear up there, nobody on the quayside that can hear what I am saying is there?"

"All clear Martin, nobody on the quayside at all, and even if there was somebody up there, they would have no chance of hearing what you are saying, I am standing right beside the phone and I can just make you out and no more, so fire away."

"Bobby I have found a sack down here filled with bottles of brandy and bottles of Advocaat. Some of them are broken but quite a few are alright, they must have been dumped over the side during a raid by Customs Officers or something like that."

"Right Martin" I answered quietly, mimicking his conspiratorial tone.

"We will send you down a clean coal sack on your lines and you can load it with the sound bottles that are left."

We filled some galvanised buckets with fresh water while Martin separated the broken bottles from the healthy ones and loaded up the coal sack. After pulling the sack aboard we removed the bottles and washed them in the buckets of fresh water then left them steeping in the buckets. Martin came aboard and after being stripped of the gear he sat looking at the haul. We had 5 bottles of Advocaat, 4 small carafe shaped bottles of 70cl Napoleon Brandy and one massive Tregnum of 3 litres of Napoleon Brandy. "Now" said Martin,

"I am taking that big bottle and one bottle of Advocaat, you can have a small bottle of Brandy and a bottle of Advocaat each and that's how it's going to be shared out, since I made the dive and found them." His tone of voice suggested he would brook no argument over the share out.

"I am going to head up to the hut now, so just bring my share up with you, when you get back to our berth."

He climbed ashore and set off walking back towards the diving hut.

"No danger of him getting caught with contraband," said George morosely.

"did you hear him, just bring my share up, when you get back to our berth."

"He is as sly as a fox," Andrew remarked.

"and if we get caught carrying his share, do you think he will own up that it is his, like hell he would."

"He has backed a loser this time anyway," I said.

"How come?" Jimmy asked.

"I had a good look at the corks on all the bottles, to see if the pressure had pressed any of them in too far. They are all sound, except the Tregnum, which must have had too big an air space between the brandy and the cork to begin with and I'm afraid the pressure has forced the cork into the bottle and probably spoilt it."

Andrew immediately picked up the Tregnum out of the pail of fresh water and sniffed at the sealed cork..

"Phew!" he remarked screwing up his face and dropping the bottle back into the pail of water.

"It smells absolutely disgusting," he said, smiling happily, "serves him right for being greedy and grabbing the lion's share, that bottle stinks with the putrid smell of silt."

"Are ours all right?" George asked, lifting out one of the small carafe shaped bottles and sniffing at the seal on top.

"I checked them all George," I assured him confidently, "They are as sound as a pound."

We set off sailing back to our own berth and the lads made no attempt to hide their enjoyment of Martin's misfortune. I found it all a bit sad the way they were carrying on, especially Andrew's continual reference to Martin's German parentage, but I suppose I should have remembered that Andrew had fought against the Germans during the war.

At 5 o'clock that evening my Dad came up the steps into the diving hut and passed Martin who was washing his upper body at the sink just inside the door. To my horror Martin said

"Oh! Hi! Arthur just let me dry myself off and I will pour you out a special drink of brandy." There was no way I could warn my Dad about the spoiled bottle, although I tried pulling faces at him and shaking my head negatively as Martin uncorked the Tregnum and poured out a good dram into a glass. He handed it to dad and re-corked the bottle and laid it back down, he then returned to the sink and carried on drying himself. Dad stared at me as I shook my head and pointed to the glass in his hand and made a face as if swallowing something horrible.

He picked up some of the message as he sniffed at the glass and then drew his nose back smartly. Martin standing at the sink had his back towards us and had not seen Dad's reaction but he said,
"You will enjoy that Arthur, the very best of Napoleon brandy." To my amazement my Dad lifted the glass on high, "Cheers Martin," he said and promptly swallowed the full glass. Still behind Martin's back, Dad shuddered and grued at the taste and motioned to me he wanted to go outside to the car. Driving home Dad said desperately,
"For God's sake stop at the Speedway Arms until I get a pint of beer to get rid of the foul taste of that brandy."

Sitting comfortably in my local bar I asked Dad,
"What possessed you to drink it?"
"Martin seemed so pleased to be giving me something special that I did not like to refuse and offend him, although now I wish I had."

The following morning Martin jumped aboard the diving boat in a wild eyed state and began raging at all of us.
"You let me go home with a bottle that was stinking worse than horse shit." he shouted loudly.
"While you buggers made off with all the good bottles, did you offer to share them with me, the man who found them in the first place, no you did not." I cut him off by shouting loudly
"HOLD IT RIGHT THERE" and Martin glared at me with hatred in his eyes.

"who was the man who gave us the wee bottles in the first place, and who said, since I found them, I am keeping the big bottle myself, **who said that Martin**?" He did not answer me but rushed off the boat and headed back towards the diving hut.

"You took the wind right out of his sails Bobby." Andrew laughed. George grinned at me as well saying.

"He does not like somebody standing up to him when he gets annoyed."

"I think he is beginning to realise he will not win many arguments against Bobby," said Jimmy.

"That's not the point Jimmy," I answered.

"I can't stand injustice of any kind, so as sure as hell he was not getting away with blaming us for the decisions he made himself. I was only sorry my poor old Dad drank a glass of that muck but at the time Martin thought it was good stuff he was giving him."

Andrew clasped his hands behind his head and leaned back against the cabin's side.

"I remember the brandy we were given in France, after we liberated the ordinary French people." he said wistfully,

"you should have tasted that, it was pure nectar."

"How long were you away from home altogether during the war Andrew?" I asked. He dropped his arms and sat forward resting his elbows on his knees.

"I was called up right at the start of the war and then found myself shipped out to Egypt with the eighth army." he said, continuing in a matter of fact way.

"when El Alamein was over I was transferred to Italy fighting the Italians and Germans at the battle of Monte Casino, after that I was transferred to France."

Andrew Imrie was a man who described his experiences without the need for embellishments, no extra glitter was added. No personal bravado to spice up his story, just the simple facts told in the most honest and convincing manner.
"Through Holland and at last into Germany, I was away from home the whole of the war, in fact it was two months after the war ended before I first came back to the U.K."
"What was it like being demobbed?" asked Jimmy.

Some inner thoughts must have passed through Andrew's mind, triggered by the question, he hesitated and a faraway look came over his eyes, then he gave a laugh.
"I landed at Southhampton and was told I had to travel all the way up to Elgin to be demobbed. It was a long haul in a train in those days and when the train stopped in Edinburgh Waverley Station it stayed there far too long for me. I was longing to see the folks, so I grabbed my kit bag and baled out of the train and away home." He laughed once more.
"I got into my civvy clothes and stuffed my uniform into a wardrobe and spent the first night at the cinema. For the next three nights I went to the dancing and was really enjoying myself."

Jimmy interrupted him once more by asking.
"Were you not worried you would get into trouble?"
Andrew puffed out his cheeks with a long exhalation of air.
"Jimmy" he said as if explaining to someone too young to understand.
"I had just come through five years of the worst trouble I was ever likely to run across in the rest of my life, but yes, in the end I did begin to worry about it and decided to go to Elgin and face the music. I dressed in my uniform and

climbed aboard a train and when I arrived at the demob centre in Elgin I said to the sentry on the gate,
"I am a wee bit late."
"No problem sergeant," said the sentry in an agreeable manner as if he was used with men arriving late.
"The sergeants mess and sleeping quarters are in the first building on the left." the sentry added, pointing out the way for me. I settled in the billet and climbed into a spare bed and fell asleep."

"In the small hours of the morning I was awakened by a torch shining in my face and standing over my bed was a tall Provo Marshall and two gaitered Military Policemen. The Provo Marshall thrust his face close to mine and snarled. "You are a wee bit late are you Imrie?" and I was hauled roughly out of bed and marched off to the guardhouse."

George had been listening to Andrew's story without passing any comment but now he asked the question that was on all of our minds.
"What punishment did they give you?" Andrew shook his head as he looked at us.
"None at all, they let me out in the morning and allowed my demob to go ahead."
"How did they let you away with that?" I asked,
"in the Navy you would have been slapped in Jankers straight away."
"When the Provo Marshall got me up out of my bed and watched me getting dressed in my uniform, as soon as I put on my blouse, their attitude changed altogether." Andrew pointed above his left breast and began numbering and explaining.

"I was wearing a ribbon for each battle campaign I had been through, The Africa Star, Monte Casino, French Legion of honour, Holland and Germany. I was carrying more decorations on my chest than Fidel Castro ever wore." He said it all in a straight forward way, without the slightest hint of boasting and finished up saying simply,
"That's what saved me."

We younger men will never know just what bitter war time memories must have been stored in Andrew's brain, causing his tremendous hatred of the German Nation as a whole, but again, complete Nations are not born evil. Their actions are the result of the corrupting influence of a few individual evil men, spreading their poison like a virulent contagious disease, until it pervades everywhere throughout a Nation, like the full Tregnum of good Brandy, corrupted and spoiled by the tiniest ingress of silt.

Chapter 25

Captain Wallace

James Wallace was one of the best known of the 'Worthies' to be found in, and around the Port of Leith and more especially within the Docks area. He was first observed as a young man, acting strangely, away back in the year 1917 and was still going strong in 1974. The passage of time never seemed to age him and even his clothes appeared to be timeless. He wore an old worsted overcoat throughout the seasons, whether hot or cold.

No one knew which sympathetic ship's officer had given him his most prized possession, but James wore his Captain's Hat with great pride. His overcoat was shabby when I first met him in 1945, I was 14 years of age and employed in Henry Robb's shipyard as a store boy, in the Joinery Department's own ironmongery store, until I was old enough to begin serving my time as a ship's joiner and cabinet maker.

James came to the serving counter of the Store one day and speaking in a deep monotonous voice, pronouncing each word slowly and deliberately he said,
"You must be Attie and Mary's boy, I used to have your Mammy sitting on my knee when she was a wee baby."

Later that evening, after telling my mother about the man I had met with the strange vacant looking eyes, she laughed and said.

"Oh! yes, that would be Captain Wallace, who lived beside us in East Cromwell street when I was young, your Granny told me he did have me on his knee when I was a baby.

All his life he has never been quite right in the head and sometimes imagines he is a great explorer like Scott of the Antarctic, but one thing he does have is a fantastic memory." Her face softened and her eyes misted over,

"as a neighbour, he was really just a poor harmless soul," she reflected.

The same old overcoat was shabbier than ever when I last saw him in 1974. From then on, it seemed no one knew what happened to him, he simply vanished. For many years he was well known around the Shipping Offices and the sailors would indulge him in a good natured way, as he recruited his crews for his phantom exploration trips around the world. Many a time my own father would tell me he had been signed on by Captain Wallace for one of his make believe Polar voyages.

Dad said the first time that happened was in 1924 and he had met him outside Christian Salvesen's offices. The self promoted Captain had a notebook and a pen in his hands. "Arthur" he had said, in his slow but deep baritone voice, "I am taking a ship down to the Antarctic later this month to try and find a new passageway through the ice and I have just signed on your friend Bob Watt to be my bosun on board, would you consider sailing with me as an Ordinary Seaman?"

"Yes eh! fine Captain you can put me down as a member of your crew, what date do we leave on?"

"My sailing time and date are still to be confirmed with the Harbour Master but I will let you know with plenty time to spare." said the Captain, as he carefully wrote Dad's name down in his little notebook.

"That's fine sir" said Dad, gripping the front of his cap as a mark of respect. He did not do that in a mocking fashion, for he told me he always treated the pseudo Officer as if he was a real ship's Captain.

Dad also told me how some people believed the Captain had lost his mind as a young ordinary seaman after being torpedoed in 1916, and some said he lost his reasoning after being kicked in the head by a horse when he was a baby and others said unkindly that he had never possessed any brains at all, from the moment of his birth. Whatever the truth was, Captain Wallace appeared to be a happy and contented man for most of the time. There were exceptions of course, when the Captain could become very angry.

One day he was walking along the timber wharves of the Victoria dock, when he came across a small cargo ship in the process of winching herself in towards the wharf. The Captain suddenly became enraged and bellowed across the water.

"You can't come in here, my ship is booked for this berth." The mate of the small coaster came hurrying out on to his bridge wing.

"Sorry sir" he called over,

"I did not know you were booked here, we will pull over to the far side."

"I should bloody well think so" roared the Captain, who was not easily appeased when he was in a temper.
"Who the hell told you, you could berth alongside here in the first place" he demanded loudly.
"I have a damned good mind to report you to the Harbour Master." The poor young Mate was distraught.
"I am terribly sorry Sir please forgive me, I had no idea you had this berth booked"
"Very well then, just get your ship to hell out of here and we will say no more about it" said the Captain magnanimously.
"Thank you Sir" the relieved mate said as he prepared to have his mooring wires transferred across the Dock to the far side.

Captain Wallace marched briskly away towards Henry Robb's shipyard, where they had humoured him, by giving him a small part time job as a Canteen cleaner.

An hour later the small coaster was again winching herself across the full width of the Dock, under the command of a young Mate who could not believe he had been fooled by an imbecile and who was still seething with rage as his ship finally came to rest alongside the wharf.

Every morning, practically at first light, the Captain would march down smartly on to the east breakwater and stand to attention facing the sea. He would then salute the open ocean and turn, in military style and march along towards the east, before turning again to face the sea and saluting once more.

He carried on all the way to Seafield in a similar manner, before coming back to the Port. Everybody knew he had in fact been torpedoed during the Great War and they said the morning ritual of saluting the empty sea was meant as a tribute to his lost shipmates.

One day at lunch time, George and I were sitting eating our midday meal in the stern of the diving boat, moored alongside our own berth at No.4 Outer Harbour. On the quayside above us stood the Captain, looking up at him, I wondered how anyone could possibly ever mistake him for a real ship's Captain. Below the scrambled egg of his Captain's hat, he wore an old faded yellow muffler around his neck and the grey and black flecked fibres of his aged worsted overcoat were bare in patches all over it. The wrinkled, seamless trouser legs, showing beneath the coat had seen much better days. A pair of down at the heel boots redeemed themselves somewhat with a cherry blossom shine, which spoke of many hours of dedicated polishing.

"We are pretty busy at the moment Captain" I said, "we have some boulders to blow up in the Leith roads Fairway today but we will make time to get the wire off your propeller for you sometime later on, where exactly is your ship moored?"

"She is lying alongside No. 8 Imperial" said the Captain in his slow, deep, sonorous voice.

"there is no real hurry diver, for we are not sailing until next tuesday but, if I am not on board when you do come, just tie in with my Chief Engineer."

It did not seem to matter to the old man that at that particular moment two tugs were assisting an eight thousand ton Ben boat to lay up at the No. 8 Imperial berth. His vivid imagination never seemed troubled by such trivialities.

"Fine Captain we will manage somehow to fit you i--- ---

A tremendous crash cut me off in mid sentence and caused us all to jump with the sudden fright. The noise had come from the Alexandra dry Dock and when we looked over there, we saw the oil rig supply vessel the East Shore, which was in the Dock at the time, appeared to have diminished somewhat in height.

This was the same ship I had burned the rope guard off two months previously, after she had run down the trawlers net and now she had been dry docked to have a new rope guard fitted, and her bottom cleaned and re-painted after completing her contract with the oil rigs.

We all rushed over there to find the ship was no longer sitting on the dry dock blocks which normally kept her keel about four foot six inches above the stone bottom of the Dock. Instead she was lying down on the stone floor, George and I were joined by the Captain, who stared down at the ship's buckled plating below her bilge line, where her hull had been bent upwards on top of the now horizontal docking blocks.

"Oh! My God" The Captain exclaimed.
"what a bloody mess, she could not have been landed level on the blocks in the first place and she has moved forward and collapsed them all. I'm afraid heads will roll over this lot."
For once the Captain was speaking sensibly and I also believed some Foremen and docking shipwrights would find themselves in deep trouble.

The following afternoon, the East Shore was floated out of the dock and moored at the Victoria entrance. We had orders to report on the full extent of the damage to her hull.

I made the dive below her and found her bottom plating was severely dented upwards every four feet approximately along the full length of her keel, where she had landed on the collapsed keel blocks.

I also marvelled at the stretch of the malleable steel she had been built with. In all of her buckled plating there was not one split in the steelwork and she remained completely watertight. Back on board the diving boat with helmet and weights removed, I sat in the stern mentally composing my report on the dreadful state of the ship's bottom.

Once again I found myself thinking over the strange relationship between Fate and Lady Luck. It seemed peculiarly uncanny to me that all the chippers and painters including Shovel chin Ritchie, wee Smithy, Tucker and Willie Velzine had come out from under the ship's bottom that day at 12-00 p.m. and were having their lunch break on top of the east end of the dry dock when the collapse occurred. Had they been still under her, they must all have perished.

Tucker told me later, that while they were having their lunch on top of the dry dock, before the collapse took place, the Captain had come over to them and asked
"Will you men be much longer in finishing the painting of my ship's bottom?" Wee Smithy, who could not suffer fools gladly, had answered the Captain saying,
"Away an' bile yer heid," but Shovel chin had quickly told Smithy to shut up and when the Captain asked politely, "What did that man say?" Tucker spoke up loudly,
"He said we will have it finished in a SHORT WHILE INDEED."

The Captain had thanked them and set off around the head of the dock towards our berth. The Chief Engineer of the East Shore was the only casualty on board. He had been in his engine room and suffered an injury to his back with the sudden drop to the dock floor. He was whisked away to Leith Hospital but thankfully made a speedy recovery.

Sitting there, thinking how close the little squad of chippers came to being killed by the ship falling on them, I looked up to find Captain Wallace standing on the quayside above me. "Diver," he called down to me in a concerned voice,
"how badly damaged is my ship, will I have to postpone my voyage to Antarctica?" I saw no reason to upset the old man by giving him the bad news of the ship's condition, especially now that it seemed to have become his latest acquisition, so I answered,

"She is fine Captain, her double bottoms are intact and she is completely watertight."
"So you can sign my Insurance Certificate and I can still sail next week as planned."
"No problem Captain," I answered, for there was nothing easier than signing the little scraps of paper that the ageing Walter Mitty carried in the deep pockets of his old overcoat
"Thank you Diver" said the Captain, and off he went, serenely happy to be in whatever parallel Universe his brain lived in.

Chapter 26

Jonathan the Terrible

I hurried down to the docks very early one morning without really knowing why I did so, after all I had expected Jonathan to return to the wild for quite some time but the sense of loss was strong within me after it finally happened and for once I found I was unable to sleep and had lain awake for a good part of the night. In the end I climbed out of bed at 4 a.m. and decided to go down to the Docks to see if he was still anywhere around.

The night before he had remained standing on the ridge of Dad's gear shed and watched the lads lock up the diving boat below him. He had never done that before, one look at them throwing the wet diving dresses up on the quayside followed by the woollen kit bags each night had always brought him hurrying down to occupy his box in the compressor room before the lads locked up the boat.

I parked the car and seeing the diving hut door wide open I walked up the steps to find out who was in there at this unearthly hour of the morning. Opening the cabin door I found Martin sitting in front of the little two bar electric fire reading a newspaper. He looked up at me as I entered and said.

"So the bird got you worried as well?"

"Yes, I could not sleep for thinking about him, but how did you manage to get a newspaper at this time of the morning."

"I didn't, this is yesterday's paper I am reading," he said folding up the newspaper and laying it down on his footstool, "when I got here I went right round to the boat to see if the bird was anywhere around."

"And was he?"

Martin smiled at my concern and the quick impatience that had caused me to cut in on him.

"Oh! He was there all right, large as life but you will never believe what he was doing." I sat down on my armchair as if I was completely relaxed and I suppose I was to some extent, knowing my boy was still around.

"So what was he doing?" I asked, opening my diving diary in a casual manner as if about to make an entry but inwardly I wanted to shake the hell out of Martin and get him to get on with it.

"He was trying to chase all the gulls off the ridge by stalking along it from one end to the other and although the gulls took off, when he reached them, they just flew around him and landed back on the end he had just left. I'll tell you Bobby he is a determined bugger for as soon as he reached the end of the shed, he turned around and started marching back again. I watched him go back and forth three times and he looked like he was prepared to keep it up all day."

"That's ma boy" I said, mimicking the cartoon bulldog in the programme Tom and Jerry on the television.

Later that morning we were leaving our berth and heading for the Imperial dry dock and Jonathan completely ignored our departure. He was too preoccupied with his new found task, and somehow he put me in mind of a vulture, as I watched him goose stepping along the shed's ridge with his head sunk between his slightly raised wing shoulders. I could understand why all the other gulls gave him a wide berth, for his appearance was the epitome of malevolence.

We arrived at the entrance to the Imperial dry dock and the lads began dressing me to make the dive. The day before Martin had used an air lift to clear all the silt out of the entrance right up to the closed gates, there being a ship in the dock. The sun was shining brightly as I slipped off the diving ladder and descended to the bottom. Martin had done a great job and I landed on completely clean stone blockwork without the usual cloud of silt boiling up around me and robbing me of all sight.

"On the bottom," I said over the phone.

"You are on the bottom," George acknowledged.

"George this is a real treat down here today, the visibility is great and the sunlight is lighting up all the colours of the rainbow coming from the marine growth."

"Sounds good" said George as I bunny hopped in towards the gates.

Row after row of large domed rivet heads came into view across the heavy plating of the gates, designed to withstand the enormous pressure of the sea. I moved along towards the hollow quoin, here the rounded vertical edge of the gate transferred that pressure into the hollowed out stonework of the quay and where steel and stone met, leaks on the inside were inevitable. Reaching the first quoin, I found myself looking at thousands of little dead bodies all the way up the quoin towards the surface. Every one of them had been sucked in tail first by the pressure and their dead eyes stared unseeingly back at me.

There were small sprats, silver eels, baby polack, codling, barbour eels, prawns, small trout and salmon parr and numerous other innocent young fish. All of them instantly the victims of a diver's worst nightmare. The thought of a barrier suddenly being opened either accidentally or on purpose between a positive and a negative pressure was something that always filled me with dread.

I stood there looking at the crushed and mutilated little bodies then turned and stared at the large rivet heads inches in front of my front light. An involuntary shudder ran through my body at the thought that only the thickness of the gate stood between my body and the negative pressure of fresh air on the inside of the dock and once more I found myself longing to be diving in the open sea again, where, irrespective of what depth we would dive to, we were always surrounded by positive pressure all around.

Casting aside the negative thoughts I lay down on the bottom to examine the bolts and the curved rails of the roller paths, which the gates wheels travelled on whilst opening or closing. Lying full length on the start of the first roller path, I pulled my toggle spanner out of my belt and began to crawl slowly along, checking that all the bolts on either side of the path were sound and tight.

Sometimes we found various solid obstructions became jammed under the gates while opening or closing and the hydraulic power of the Rams would be so strong that the obstructions would shear off some of the bolts and it was our job to replace them.

My front light was about twelve inches above the roller path as I crawled along checking everything was in good order. Small to medium sized crabs ran side on away from me and small fish tried to satisfy their curiosity by peering in through my helmet's side and front lights. Suddenly I was confronted by one of the strangest sights I ever saw underwater.

In the centre of the roller path and facing towards me was a young prawn, a very brave young prawn and one who did not know the meaning of the word fear. His attitude told me there was no danger he was going to give way to me. Less than a foot above him towered my helmet, backed up by almost four hundred weight of man and diving gear, yet was he intimidated by the sight, like hell he was.

He raised himself up on his tiny front legs and darted forward around about three inches menacingly, he was most obviously trying to chase me off the roller path. He retreated by the same distance when I refused to get excited by his bluff. Deciding he could not get me to back up or move sideways off the roller path he settled down and spread out all of his little legs in an attitude of, 'He shall not pass'.

I thrust my helmet three inches closer towards him quickly, in a threatening manner, and again he raised himself on his front legs and to my utter amazement he opened his tiny jaws as wide as he could and offered to bite me.

"Don't be so God damned stupid" I said aloud.
"Who are you talking to?" George asked over the phone, and I told him what was happening and finished up saying.
"You won't believe this George, he is less than two inches long and with his mouth wide open it is lucky if it is any more than one quarter of an inch in diameter, yet he is

offering to swallow me up whole, or at least bite the hell out of me. All my life I have always said I like a trier but honestly George this wee chappy pleases me far too much."

Having said that, I used one bare hand to usher my tiny but brave opponent gently to one side, well clear of the roller path so I did not accidentally crush him as I passed by, then I carried on and completed my examination and repair of the roller path rails and their bolts.

Before leaving the dry dock that night we collected a fair amount of small sprats and herring from the sieves of the dry Dock's pumps then set off back to our own berth. Arriving there we found nothing had changed other than the fact that Jonathan seemed to have given up his persecution of the other gulls, for he was now sitting alone on the east end of the shed's ridge and allowing the rest of the gulls to occupy the centre without attacking them.

I carried a plate of the sprats out of the boat's cabin and tossed them up on the quay. Down came the gulls, like a fusillade of bullets and Jonathan let out a scream of anger and left the ridge and hurtled in amongst them on the quayside.

"My God" said Andrew, watching his aggression,
"he fights like a tiger." The fish were all gone in a flash and the gulls retreated back up onto the ridge but Jonathan remained on the quay, glaring balefully at me.
"I don't think he likes you anymore," said George,
"now that you have started feeding the rest of the gulls." I looked at my boy and noted his tail feathers were now almost as long as any of the other bird's tails and I realised

once they were fully grown I would not be able to tell him apart from any of the other adult male Herring gulls.

"He has to learn to fend for himself whether he likes it or not," I said.

"Fend for himself," Andrew laughed, pointing up at Jonathan who had taken off and was once more attacking the main body of gulls on the roof.

"It's the other birds I feel sorry for, because it's really a case of dog eat dog life, all the time among seagulls and that bugger is like a Rottweiler among Chihuahuas."

I looked up at Jonathan and somehow I felt that Andrew was right. He was slowly marching along in his stiff legged goose step towards the rest of the birds and was once more wearing his mantle of a look-alike vulture. The gulls were taking off individually as he came towards them, but instead of returning to the other end of the roof, they were all wheeling away towards the Western Harbour.

"I think they have all had enough of his violence" said Jimmy.

"it looks like they are clearing out altogether."

"Almost" said Andrew pointing up once more. The remaining birds had lifted up in a body and followed the others towards the West, all but one,

"see, there's one left that's not afraid of him."

The gull left standing on the roof was slightly smaller and slimmer than Jonathan and it stood perfectly still and watched his sinister approach until he was no more than three feet away from it, then in an unconcerned way, it turned its head away from him and looked in the opposite direction altogether. Jonathan stopped dead in his tracks and his body language appeared to say. 'Who is this upstart who dares to challenge Jonathan the Terrible?' His head and neck emerged from between the hunched up wing shoulders and he stood bolt upright and turning his bill up to the sky he opened up that gaping mouth of his and gave forth a loud prolonged raucous cry.

The other gull was obviously unimpressed with this demonstration for it did not deign to turn its head back in his direction. I could now see my boy was sorely perplexed by the strange gull's complete disregard of him and he was obviously uncertain what he should try next against such a strong willed, fearless opponent.

While he pondered the situation the other gull turned towards him, pointed its bill at the sky and opened its mouth wide and out poured a more melodious cry. The effect on Jonathan was truly amazing, he turned his head side on as if listening intently to the softer, higher tones of the other bird's voice and all the aggression left him immediately.

"Ha!" said Andrew,
"that'll do now, he has found himself a girl friend." Andrew was right and Jonathan had indeed found himself a girl friend. We watched them begin billing and cooing for some time until I had to leave the boat and go up to the diving hut to fill in my daily diving diary once again.

Over the next several days Jonathan and his Lady occupied the ridge of the shed during the daytime and in the evenings they made it their nightime roosting place. I fed them during this time and Jonathan was a perfect gentleman and offered her sprats to eat in such a timid and gentle manner that it encouraged other gulls to try their luck in an approach. They were in for a bit of a shock, for woe betide any other male who dared to come anywhere near his Lady.

We were now at the end of the month of April and because of my boyhood experience of bird nesting I realised Jonathan and his lady friend were completely smitten with each other and I knew they would be leaving us pretty soon, for the bigger birds always began nesting during the month of May.

The following morning they returned to the ridge after I had fed them and there, they settled down to digest their breakfast. The lads came aboard followed by Martin and we prepared to set sail for Granton Harbour.

We had orders to find and remove a small boulder which had been reported sticking up above the seabed inside the berths of the lighthouse ships the Hesperus and the Pharos. The intention was to sling the boulder on to a stone barge using the Digger, rather than using explosives inside the area of such a small harbour.

Just before we left our berth that morning, Jonathan and his Lady took to the wing and flew off in a northerly direction. I watched them keep going until they both looked like two tiny specks of dust in the sky and although I never saw them again, I took comfort in the thought that they had gone off to start a new life together and most probably to raise a family of their own.

Chapter 27

Brandy Galore

Immediately after Jonathan and his Lady vanished from our sight George and I were standing by ourselves in the stern of the boat as we sailed towards Granton Harbour, the rest of the diving team were in the cabin and out of earshot.
"I was in my local bar the Speedway Arms last night," I said quietly to George,
"when Johnny Gaffney, the docker came in and drew me to one side to talk to me."

"I'm told you have a job on tomorrow in Granton," he had said almost in a whisper, as he looked all around him in a furtive manner, as if he was making sure no one close by was listening. His cloak and dagger manner rubbed off on me and I found myself answering in a similar quiet whisper.
"That's right, we have to remove a boulder from the Light Ship's berth, you know, where the Hesperus and the Pharos usually lie up when they come in."

"Right" he said and moved his head closer to my ear and began speaking quietly out of the side of his mouth.
"one of the crew aboard a merchant ship lying alongside the West pier was smuggling brandy for a bar owner in Leith." he hesitated and looked all around himself again. I was a bit

apprehensive of what kind of skulduggery he was attempting to get me involved in, as he whispered.

"No names, no pack drill, get what I mean Rab but he decided to carry it all ashore at midnight one night last week and he was in the middle of the Gangway when a car drew up with a screech of brakes, and in the dim lighting of the pier he saw men scrambling out of the car and caught sight of uniforms and he thought it was Customs men in a raid on his ship so he dropped the whole lot over the side. It wasn't until after he had ditched it, he found out it was his own drunken Officers coming back from a run ashore."

"What did he throw over the side?" I found myself whispering excitedly in anticipation.

"Around about fifty full sized bottles of napoleon brandy." said Johnny, and I whisled in appreciation. "Shoosh" he said in alarm, fearful I might draw attention to us.

"anyway, I drew a cross on the edge of the timber wharf directly above the spot the lot went in, so if you are going there tomorrow, you might want to have a look for it."

George had listened to the story without comment but after a few minutes of consideration he said doubtfully.

"It's Martin who is diving today and he always says he is not interested in wild goose chases after ditched contraband, so I don't think he will be easily persuaded to have a look for it."

"Don't worry George" I answered with confidence,
"I will persuade him."

"Oh! Oh!" George exclaimed quietly.
"talk of the Devil and he is sure to appear," as Martin stepped out of the cabin and joined us in the stern of the

boat. We were rising and falling to the action of a strong following ground swell and Martin gripped hold of the brackets which held up our coiled air hoses, to steady himself against the boat's movement. He turned and looked over towards Newhaven as we were passing the small boat harbour mouth.

There were quite a few small yachts and cabin cruisers moored inside the harbour and Martin began slowly shaking his head from side to side as if he was appraising them and was unhappy with what he was seeing.

"Looking at that lot I reckon we burned quite a few far better boats among the ones we took out of the Old Dock," he said. George's face hardened and his eyes glittered.

"That was a bloody shame," he growled fiercely, "if I had owned one of the boats they made us destroy I would have sued the Commission."

If anything George contrived to look even more menacing as he continued.

"nowadays I'm beginning to really hate the Bosses and the idle rich who get themselves in positions of power and lord it over us, as I see it, they do very little to earn their own corn but they have plenty to say about how we earn ours and try their best to keep us on a minimum wage all the time." He jumped down from the transom and into the cabin in obvious anger.

"Well that certainly got George in a temper," Martin said leaning both elbows on the cabin roof to steady himself, as I altered the boat's course across the swell.

"Yes but not so wild as last Saturday" I said pointing the boat's head directly at the mouth of Granton Harbour.

"Why, what happened then?" Martin asked and I told him the story:

"Dad, George and I were fishing for trout on the river Tyne, up in Pencaitland, above Haddington and on the Saturday afternoon the sun was high in the sky and its heat was bordering on the oppressive. Water levels were low and the warmed river water flowed with a greatly reduced rate. The trout lay doggo, like crocodiles, they were conserving their energy as they awaited the coolness of the evening before coming back on the take again."

"George was walking along the river bank when he happened to notice what looked like some old junk glinting in the sunlight from deep within a nearby copse of trees, which was well away from the river. He left the river bank and walked over and into the trees and came upon an illegally dumped pile of rubbish. He noticed small pieces of copper and brass among the scattered debris and since the trout had gone off the take, George had lost interest in the fishing and instead he began collecting the non ferrous metal. He was busily searching through the rubbish when a voice spoke up behind him."

"What ah you doing he-ah?" George turned around to find a middle aged man frowning sternly at him. The man wore the garb of a landed country gentleman, in the form of plus four trousers above a pair of very expensive looking heavy brogue shoes, which looked completely at odds compared with an old Captain's army jacket worn above them.

"You have no wight to be he-ah, this is my land." The man's inability to pronounce any word properly that contained the letter 'R' was the first thing that George noticed about his would-be snobbish speech, as the man berated him.

"What ah you doing he-ah on my land?"

"I was fishing for trout and noticed this dumped stuff in among the trees and I just came over for a look." George explained in a reasonably quiet manner, although he felt himself becoming annoyed at the other man's arrogant way of talking down to him.

"I don't mind you fishing fo-ah twout in the wivah, have you got a pehmit to fish fo-ah twout."

"Yes" George answered, without bothering to produce it.

"I always have a permit every time I go fishing."

"Well as I said I don't mind people staying on the bank of the wivah if they ah fishing, but not leaving the wivah and coming in heah. The-ah no twout he-ah and this is my land and you ah on it without my pehmmision," he said in a lofty manner. George felt a real anger start rising within him and although he normally showed a quiet disposition for most of the time and would rather do a man a good turn than do him a bad turn, he could be quick to react, If he felt someone was talking down to him.

"How is it your land?" he suddenly demanded aggressively. The other man was taken aback and his mouth hung open at such an outrageous question, then gathering himself somewhat he said.

"You ah on the land of Stevensons Policies and I am Captain Stevenson and this is my land." George thrust his jaw out in a threatening manner and took a step nearer to the Captain.

"How did you get this land in the first place?" he growled

The Captain took a step backwards away from the implied violence as he tried to grasp the import of the last question, then he stood bolt upright and declared loudly.

"This land has belonged to my family fo-ah many hundweds of ye-ahs, in fact fo-ah many centu-ahways," he carried on arrogantly. "My ancesto-ahs had to fight fo-ah this land."

"Right" said George balling up his two fists and immediately adopting a boxing stance.

"I will fight you for it now."

"Oh! My God" the horrified Captain exclaimed as he hurried away. Martin laughed aloud as I finished the story.

"George would do that right enough, in a minute," he said as he looked ahead of the boat at the mouth of Granton harbour directly in front of us.

"I better start getting dressed," he said stepping inside the cabin and sitting down on the dressing stool, where George had his woollens laid out in readiness.

I steered the boat through the Harbour mouth and turned her towards the east pier where I could see the tug Oxcar and the Digger lying alongside the wharf. I took her in alongside of the Digger and made her fast. Bunty, the skipper of the Digger was watching me tie her up. He stood on his deck with both elbows behind him and the backs of his hands resting on his hips. I knew that stance well and it meant Bunty was in a cantankerous mood.

"Where the hell have you been, I want to get the bloody stone up out of here and get back to my own work in Leith." He shouted over at me. I did not answer him and he stood there with a look on his face as if he had just swallowed a tot of pure malt vinegar. Martin came out of the cabin fully dressed except for weights and helmet.

"Aye and I want you to get back to Leith as well and get some of that silt removed from the Docks."

The Digger's normal every day's work was to use its bucket grab and fill mud barges to be taken away and dumped at sea to lower the overall level of silt and rubbish throughout the docks.

"Well then, the sooner you get that rock up, the sooner I can leave" said Bunty as he turned away and walked into his Deck Housing. Martin finished dressing and went down to find the boulder, while I thought of nothing else but all that good brandy lying on the bottom beside the west pier.

Granton harbour was a much smaller and shallower Port than Leith and I was pretty sure the bottle's corks would not be forced into them by the reduced pressure of less depth.

"Aw! Its only a tiny wee thing" Martin's voice came over the diver phone. I glanced at his depth guage which was reading 22 feet of an ebbing tide.

"It has a fresh score across its top probably done recently by a ship's keel."

"Got that Martin, what size of wire do you need?" George asked.

"I won't be able to get a wire around it George because its saddle shaped and the bottom all around it is solid." I moved to the phone.

"How high is it above the bottom Martin?"

"It is lucky if it is any more than two feet above the bottom but I can't sling it so I will have to bore and Rawl bolt it."

"Right Martin do you want us to send you down the rock drill?"

"Aye, send it down and get a 12 inch by one and a half inch eyed Rawl Bolt ready for me"
"Got that Martin will do" I said and turned the phone over to George again.

While Martin was drilling into the boulder, I was watching the tall slim figure of Bunty back out on his deck. He had once more taken up his aggressive stance of backs of hands on hips and elbows thrusting out behind him. On his head he wore an all black Captain's hat above a blue boiler suit and the vinegar look was firmly back in its place as he watched the air erupting from Martin's rock drill. He and I had practically ignored each other since we had the altercation at the time I had set off the big charge ordered by Mr. De Vries, the one that shook the hell out of his Digger.

Safely on board after hooking the Digger on to the rawl bolt Martin called across to Bunty.
"Ok Bunty you can take her away," Bunty signalled to his crane driver to heave up. The steam pistons of the crane rattled away at speed to start with then began slowing down dramatically, we watched in disbelief as the Digger began listing heavily.
"Whoa" Bunty roared in alarm followed instantly by,
"Lower away"and the crane driver eased the Digger back down on to an even keel.
"What in God's name have you hooked us on to?" Bunty demanded in a fit of rage. Martin stared at the Skipper and described something very small with both hands.
"Its just a wee boulder" he said.
"no more than 3 feet long by 2 feet high and two feet wide."

"Rubbish" Bunty shouted loudly as he marched across his deck towards us. He stopped and pointed down at the water beneath his crane.

"You can get down there Martin and free my bloody hook, a wee boulder is it," he said sarcastically.

"Its more like you have hooked us on to half the Granton foreshore so let my hook go so I can get back to Leith and get on with my own work."

It was now Martin's turn to look angry but he did not argue with Bunty and returned to the bottom and released the crane's hook. Bunty wasted no time in securing his crane and organising the tug Oxcar to take the Digger in tow, so we cast off our own boat and moored at the quay and watched them head off towards Leith.

Martin was still showing signs of anger when he sat down on the dressing stool and said rather wearily.

"Take the gear off George because I can't do any more without the Digger"

"Martin could you keep the suit on for a special job for ourselves?"I asked him.

"What special job for ourselves?" he asked in a disinterested voice.

"I happen to know where we could possibly lay our hands on a fair number of bottles of brandy." I said.

"Where about is this brandy?" he sighed looking at me with bored, lack lustre eyes.

"Over by the West Pier." I said and I was instantly startled by Martin's reaction as he suddenly shouted loudly.

"Not on your fucking life, I'm not going raking all over Granton Harbour searching for phantom bottles that everybody knows are not there. I have spent God knows how many hours searching for non existing booze in the past, and it was always originally reported as having been recently dumped here, there and every fucking where and never once did I ever find anything. George, take the gear OFF."

The start of his tirade triggered rage in me and the length of it brought things to a head as I exploded.

"Right George take his fucking gear OFF and GET ME DRESSED IN MINE for we are having that brandy." This was only the second time Martin had ever seen me in a rage since I became his diving buddy but he himself was not a man who backed down easily and his eyes bored into mine as he said pointedly,

"There's no time left for a changeover for I want to get back to our own berth early today."

"Well that is just too bad Martin because if you are not going to dive it, I certainly will."

He turned his eyes away from the intensity of my glaring and stared blankly at George for quite a while, before deciding to give way by saying.

"Ok George I will dive it, but only because I am already dressed and we would lose too much time in a change over, so we better get over there now, for the quicker I prove there is nothing there the better, and the quicker we can set off back to Leith."

I took the helm and we moved over to the west pier and finding a fairly large Merchant ship lying in the berth, I moored our boat close to her stern. I then climbed up on the wharf and began walking alongside the ship, focussing my eyes on the timber edge of the wharf. Almost half way along the length of the ship I came upon it, a clearly defined cross that had been scribed into the top member of the timber wharf.

I walked back to the boat and collected the shot weight, retraced my steps to the telltale cross and lowered the shot very, very gently to the bottom. I did not want to break anything that might be lying down there.

Returning on board the boat I made the shot line fast to the diving ladder. George lifted Martin's helmet over his head and the bitching and moaning of the diver came over the phone as he sank down to the bottom.

"You know George I don't understand why I listen to Bobby and let him talk me into all this nonsense. Anyway I am on the bottom George."

"You are on the bottom Martin" said the linesman as he smiled and winked at me.

"I suppose no one knows better than you do George how often I have done this in the past and never once found anything."

"That's true Martin, I've lost track of how many times you have tried searching for stuff the Dockers told us was on the bottom and never found anything." said George, again grinning at me and winking once more.

"Of course its me that is the stupid bugger for giving in to him and coming down here in yet another Wild Goo"

His voice cut off abruptly and we were left listening to the sound of just his bubbles over the phone. George cocked an ear towards the set as the silence persisted then he slowly pretended to yawn.

"Something bothering him again" he said and as he spoke Martin exclaimed.

"Oh! Oh! God, George put Bobby on the phone,"
"Right Martin" said George offering the set to me with a one handed gesture. I depressed the speak switch.
"Go ahead Martin,"
"Bobby I've found dozens of big bottles here in a pile and although some of them are broken there are plenty others completely undamaged, what should I do?"
"Martin hang fire and we will send you down a sugar sack on your lines."

Shortly after that with Martin aboard and stripped of the diving gear, I took the helm and we set off for Leith, while the lads and Martin washed and dried our haul of large brandy bottles. By the time we arrived back at our own Berth Martin had decided on the share out. There were 36 bottles in all, sealed and protected by sound corks. It was to be 10 bottles to Martin, 8 to me and 6 each to George, Andrew and Jimmy. The lads were most unhappy with the share out and if possible it made their hatred of Martin greater than ever before.

Three weeks later a knock came on the diving hut door while I was filling in the diving diary and Martin walked out of our cabin to answer it. From inside the cabin I heard voices raised in anger at the front door and although I could not hear what was being said I knew someone was livid over something or other. The front door slammed shut and Martin came back into the cabin scowling.
"What was that all about?" I asked him.
"That was the bar owner the brandy was supposed to go to and he started kicking up hell with me."

"What was he saying?"

"He said he had paid for the whole lot and he had just found out we managed to get some of it back from the bottom of the dock and he wanted it now."

"What did you tell him?"

"I told him if he had come here three weeks ago he might have had a chance of getting something back but now it has all been drunk up and I slammed the door in his face."

Chapter 28

Lightships Granton

"The Captain of the Pharos has lodged an official complaint and we must act on it immediately," said Captain Childs. "We have to remove it, one way or the other Martin."
For the first time I noticed the young Deputy Harbour Master showing real concern over an issue coming up during his watch.
"Well I tried my best Captain, the rock looked so small I thought all I had to do was hook the Digger on to it but Bunty said it was too heavy for the Digger, so what else could I do?" Martin said, adroitly side stepping the blame for failure.
"Can we blow it up with explosives?" the Captain asked and Martin turned the question aside by looking directly at me for an answer.
"I have not seen it myself Captain." I answered,
"although it was obvious to all of us it was too heavy for the Digger and the probable reason must be, that it extends well below the sea bed but to answer your question, inside such a small Harbour with timber wharves I could only use small amounts of gelatin dynamite at any one time, so I think we

should be allowed to work on it for two or three days before you send the Digger back to try again."

"Right lads" said the Captain showing a more relaxed attitude now that there was a definite course of action he could take.

"I will phone David Grieve and tell him you will be working in Granton until that boulder has been removed and we will keep the Digger working here in Leith until you are ready for it." We took our leave of the Deputy Harbour Master and the Tug Oxcar towed our barge back to Granton Harbour.

I dressed and made the dive. The water of the flowing tide was crystal clear and I found myself looking at the small boulder Martin had described fairly accurately. It was about 3 feet long and 2 feet wide and stood about 2 feet above a hard level bottom. I found I could not penetrate the sea bed beside it with a small hand pick-axe I had taken down with me, it was so hard. The eyed Rawl bolt was in place in the top of the boulder and showed signs of being stretched with the strain of the Digger's pull, which made me realise there must be a far bigger percentage of the boulder below the sea bed than above.

For the next two days Martin and I drilled a series of one and a half inch diameter holes all around it's base, downwards into it at an angle of about 60 degrees inwards towards it's centre. On the third day, no longer requiring our barge, now the stone drilling was completed, we sailed our boat to Granton accompanied by the Oxcar. We always had a tug boat with us when using explosives.

I took the dive and stemmed every second hole with tiny quarter pound shots of gelatin dynamite to a total of 2 pounds in all. We now had to have the Duke of Buccleuch's permission to fire, as the Harbour was still privately owned by him at that time. We were introduced to the Duke's foreman Carpenter, a man by the name of Drummond Gillies, who assured us he had been entrusted with overseeing the whole operation. This small, sturdily built, grey haired man exhuded an unbelievable arrogance while talking to us and finished up ordering us to do no more until he came back.

After he left Martin said,

"I've had a few run ins with that 'Curly' Gillies, he is a proper bastard of a man and full of his own importance, I'm going up to have a word with the harbour Master about him." After Martin left the boat Andrew said,

"Bendicks does not realise that he and 'Curly Gillies' are two of a kind, both of them are as arrogant as hell but at least 'Curly' has a bit of intelligence."

"I don't like any of the two of them," said George

"they both have the same habit of talking down to us as if we were nothing."

"A couple of years ago," said Jimmy passing out freshly made cups of coffee.

"Bendick's said the day would come when he would punch 'Curly' in the mouth."

"Bendicks should realise that he is closing towards sixty years of age and his fighting days are over," said Andrew wisely.

At lunchtime that day I sat in the cabin with the lads, eating the midday meal that Jimmy had cooked for us, while Martin remained outside sitting on the top of the cabin roof and apparently quite happy to make do with a small handful of raisins for his meal. I was now seeing for myself that Martin would never condescend to eat with the rest of the team, exactly as they had told me previously. I thought once again of the Upstairs Downstairs syndrome and smiled as I considered I was sitting with the servants down below while the master sat regally alone above us. I was still musing over this comical simile, when Martin rushed in past us and opened the compressor room door and hurriedly stepped inside and crouched down behind the diving compressor.

Almost simultaneously there came a call from the quayside above us.

"Diving boat" it was 'Curly' Gillies's voice.

"Go out and see him" Martin whispered insistently, motioning me outside with frantic gestures of both hands. I glanced at the clock, it was 1-10 p.m. dinner time was over, so I stepped out into the stern and looked up at 'Curly' on the timber wharf above me.

"Is that stoy marking the position of the boulder?" he asked pointing to the orange buoy about twenty feet out from the wharf.

"It is" I answered

"How much gelignite are you going to fire?"

"Oh! It's very small, only 2 pounds in total." He laughed and his shoulders shook as he remarked derisively.

"Two pounds in total, well, if that is all it is, you can fire it right now."

"No I can't, I must get the Harbour Master's permission first and also move the boat away a safe distance before I can fire it." He shook his head in a derogatory fashion as if two pounds of explosives were of no consequence whatsoever and I was making a mountain out of a mole hill.

I called the lads out to shift the boat and asked the Oxcar skipper to confirm I had the Harbour Master's permission to fire at 1-30 p.m. Martin remained hidden in the compressor room as the lads moved the boat well down the pier, while I paid out the electrical wires attached to the detonators. When all was ready I called back to 'Curly' who was still standing in the same place on the edge of the wharf, no more than twenty feet from the boulder's position.

"Drummond, move away, I can't fire with you standing there."

"Oh! For God's sake, fire your pop gun and be done with it." he called back in a disgusted voice.

"Go on Bobby" Andrew said behind me,

"fire it and to hell with the stubborn bugger"

"Drummond I have less than five minutes left, to fire this shot on time and if you don't move away now, then you will force me to cancel until tomorrow and I will be duty bound to report the reason why I did not set it off on time."

That did it, he turned away from the water's edge and began walking ever so slowly towards us.

"1-30 exactly on the dot," George said, monitoring the time for me and although 'Curly' was still on the timber work, I fired. The timber jetty shook violently and whipped the legs out from under the obstinate foreman and landed him on his bottom. He scrambled back on his feet and marched up to our boat saying loudly and angrily,

"That was far more than two pounds of gelignite you fired."

I saw George's face take on its customary hard look when anyone challenged the truth as he knew it.

"Well I don't know where he got the rest from," he said aggressively.

"Because Andrew and I gave him down exactly eight small quarter pound sticks of jelly and no more." Without another word the irate foreman turned and stomped away.

The following morning we were back in Granton and shortly after we arrived the Oxcar towed the Digger in through the harbour entrance. Martin dressed and went down to have a look at the result.
"Put Bobby on the phone"
"Right Martin" said George, laughing at the antics of Andrew, who had immediately taken up a boxing stance and with both small fists raised he was threatening the voice coming up from the sea bed.
 "Go ahead Martin" I said,
   "The sixteen holes we bored have a wide crack running through the centre of them, all the way around the rock, do you think it will lift away now?"
Bunty, standing on the deck of the digger alongside us heard him.
"Don't tell me he brought us back here without knowing whether the bloody thing will come up or not." He spat over the side as if trying to remove an evil taste from his mouth and walked away into his deck housing, shaking his head in disgust.
"With any luck it should come away Martin, after all we did bore inwards towards its centre." I said optimistically.
"Ok send down the crane"
"Crane coming down now" said George signalling to the driver to lower away.

With the crane hooked on to the eyed rawl bolt and Martin back on board divested of weights and helmet, he called over to the driver to,

"Take her up." The steam crane hissed and rattled as it took the strain and once more the digger began listing heavily.

"Whoa" Bunty roared in an alarmed tone of voice, as he broke into a run towards the crane cabin, motioning downwards with one hand.

"Lower away" "Lower away" he repeated frantically as the crane driver eased off the load and brought the digger back on an even keel.

Bunty turned to face Martin and threw out both his arms in a gesture of dismissal.

"That's it finished" he shouted,

"We are out of here now and we are not coming back until you are sure the bloody thing is liftable."

"For God's sake Bunty give it a chance" Martin screamed in desperation at the prospect of another failure.

"I've given it all the chance I am going to give it and that's final." the cantankerous old skipper yelled at Martin.

"You are quite right Bunty" I shouted across, and I was instantly aware of the murderous look Martin directed towards me before I continued,

"you are right to give up, for your bloody old crane is past it nowadays and could not haul snow off a dyke, it won't be long before the Commission realise it too, and retire the Digger along with you and your crew."

Bunty's face turned a deep purple and he screamed at his crane driver to heave up and as soon as the diggers list became too pronounced he called to lower away again, then heave up once more. At the third attempt the boulder top gave way and the digger leapt upwards a fair height and began see-sawing violently up and down, sending quite sizeable waves in towards the shore.

The crane driver was still heaving up and the whole crew of the Digger, including Bunty joined in hysterical laughter when the boulder top came up above the surface. The eyed rawl bolt had a grip of the smallest boulder we had ever set eyes on. It was about 2 feet x 2 feet x 9 inches thick with the bottom half of the rawl bolt protruding below it.

To be fair to the irascible old skipper, his craft had almost ripped a monster of a boulder out of the hard bottom before the top half of it collapsed altogether in pieces leaving only its tip still hanging from the crane. Martin returned to the bottom and reported a mass of shattered stone in a hole where the boulder had been. All of it small enough for the digger to lift away with its large grab and this was done.

Back at our berth, Martin left us as usual and once more the lads began to belittle him.

"What do you think of the man that was going to punch 'Curly' in the mouth now?" asked Andrew. "hiding in the compressor room like a craven coward."

"Aye but he got in a worse state when Bunty said he was going to give up on the job again," said George,

"he was almost crying with rage and looked like he would have strangled Bunty if he could have reached him."

Jimmy tapped me on the knee saying, "You don't know it Bobby but he almost turned on you when it seemed you were agreeing with Bunty to begin with."

"I noticed all right Jimmy but I was too busy baiting Bunty in order to get him in such a rage he would have another go at it."

From that day onwards Martin and I were on Bunty's list of his least favourite people.

Chapter 29

Pixie and the White Stuff

"Now Bobby son, I hope you are eh! hope you are remembering to keep Martin Bendicks eh! keep Martin out of your explosives magazine." David Grieve said forcefully that morning, as if this new job for Edmund Nuttal involving explosives had re-awakened some special fear in his mind.
"I have not forgotten David but I wish you would tell me why?"
"Never mind why, just don't eh! don't let Martin touch explosives eh! don't let him touch them at all."
 As an ex Petty Officer in the Royal Navy this sounded like a direct order to me and one I would be unable to obey.
"David I have to let Martin touch explosives, he has to take the charges down, because I can't be in two places at the same time."
His eyebrows met each other in the centre of his forehead as he tried to follow what I meant and his hands began absently tidying up the blank papers lying in front of him on his desk.
"Aye well, as long as you keep him eh! keep him away from the eh! from your magazine, but this job is for Edmond

Nuttal so I suppose they will be eh! they will be supplying their own explosives Bobby son." He picked up his pen and looked down at the papers on his desk. This was again my cue he was finished with me and I turned and left his office.

On my way round to the diving boat I came upon Eddie Connelly and his men laying new cobble stones between the Railway lines alongside the Tug berth. Eddie saw me coming and up went his right boot and stamped down hard on the ground and he twisted his foot from side to side, violently grinding its leather sole into the cobbles.

"Don't forget Bob get a foothold on everybody's nose to get yourself higher up the ladder of success in this life." He shouted over, grinning broadly at me. I gave him a wave as I passed by and answered him by calling back.

"Don't worry Eddie I won't forget." This morning everybody seemed to be exhorting me not to forget something or other and it reminded me of cousin Dod Donaldson's favourite saying when leaving someone after arranging a date, by shouting back at them,

"Don't forgot now," the improper use of the past tense always amused him.

When I climbed on board the diving boat I found the team all present except for Martin and I had discovered in the past he did not like it when David Grieve sent for me instead of him, when any special job requiring explosives turned up. His protest was always shown by having us wait for him, for he deliberately arrived late every time it happened.

The water of Leith was in spate and running quite briskly alongside of our moored boat. It followed its own course until it passed under the large swing bridge up stream from us, then it's muddy brown water swirled around the basin where we lay and passed our boat quite quickly, before merging once more with the main river downstream. Martin jumped aboard and exclaimed loudly.

"Oh! For God's sake the poor wee thing."

He jumped up on the narrow walkway that ran from the cockpit to the bow along the side of the cabin and he hung on one handed to the hand rail mounted on the cabin top. This brought us all outside to find out what was exciting him.

Coming around the basin and desperately low in the turbulent water was a tiny kitten. It's paws were barely managing to hold it's head above the fast moving frothing current as it was carried past the two dry docks and swinging around it approached our boat at real speed.

Hanging on with the one hand Martin knelt down on the narrow 9 inch belting that formed the walkway around the cabin of the boat and as the kitten flew past him he scooped the drowning mite out of the maelstrom.

He let out a howl of pain as he desperately tried to regain the safety of the cockpit and to his everlasting credit he hung on to the baby animal grimly, while it tore his wrist to shreds with a fast disembowelling action of both hind legs and sunk it's tiny but razor sharp teeth into his thumb again and again. He jumped into the cockpit past the three of us and dropped the terrified kitten inside the open door of the cabin. If I had never understood what was meant by the saying, 'as fast as a scalded cat' I certainly did now as the kitten flew through the cabin and vanished instantly into the compressor room.

Instead of using the boat's First Aid Box Martin left us and returned to the diving hut to attend to his wounds. Try as hard as we could, none of the three of us could work out exactly where the kitten was hiding, although it soon became pretty obvious to us it was so small it had somehow managed to get itself down into the bilges under the engine of the compressor but at least we knew it would be perfectly safe down there.

Martin returned to the boat with his right hand bandaged up and although it was his turn to make the dive, I knew he would never ask what the job was, instead he sat down on the dressing stool and began discussing the rescue of the small black and white kitten. His taciturn nature would not allow him to ask for information of any kind from any member of the diving team. I found this a singularly strange part of Martin's make up whereby he seemed to feel it was beneath his dignity to ask any questions at all regarding our work.

I took the helm and we sailed round to the Imperial basin, while George began laying out Martin's woollens. We arrived where the main Contractor Edmund Nuttal had a small secondary job, a few hundred yards further in shore than the construction of the New Locks, which were ongoing inside the Cellular Dam.

We moored up alongside the inshore lead-in stone quay and Martin surprised me by coming out of the cabin wearing only the standard suit, no boots or corselet.

"So it's an outside contract?" he said, more like a statement of fact than a question.

"Yes it's for Nuttal," was my ultra short reply. Martin must have decided to show he was completely unconcerned by my not giving him any further information about the job as he began leaning against the diving ladder's stringers and gazing at Nuttal's men working above him on the quay. He remained like that with his back facing us as the minutes went by and Andrew looked at me and shook his head sadly.

Nuttal's Foreman appeared above us, the same man who had been in charge of the small cofferdam at the time of the Big Blow.

"Diver would you like to come up and have a word with Alfred Noble's man,?" he asked. Martin looked up at him with the same determined scowl on his face.

"Yes I will be with you in a few minutes," he said and looked back down at the water around the bottom of the ladder.

He remained like that, leaning with both elbows on the tops of the ladder stringers with his head bowed and staring blankly at the water below him, until the Foreman shook his head and walked away. The whole incident was becoming increasingly embarrassing until he finally looked around at me and asked.

"Who the hell is this Nobleman Alfred?"in the same arrogant tone of voice.

"He will be one of Alfred Noble's explosive experts I suppose," I answered,

"wanting to have a discussion with you about what he wants you to blow up for him."

If I thought for one moment that this would bring Martin out of his mood then I was mistaken as he said.

"Oh! In that case YOU better go up and see him," and he made it sound like a direct order as he walked back into the cabin to finish dressing. I climbed ashore remembering what Andrew had said some time ago.

"You know Bobby, ignorance is bad enough but ignorance coupled with arrogance is ten times worse," how right Andrew was.

I returned to the boat with the explosive expert and we passed down four bags of submarine gelatine, each bag had it's own run of cordtex detonating fuse running down into it, to set them off individually with a split second timing in between, to lessen the effect of the shock waves.

We left the explosive expert on the east side and sailed slowly over to the second lead-in quay wall, trailing the four runs of cordtex behind us. I explained to Martin he would have to place each bag at the base of the wall directly underneath each of the four separate marks on the top of the wall which the Alfred Noble man had measured out, and hold the bags in place there, by loading them with broken stonework lying on the bottom.

Martin stood on the diving ladder and we gave him the first bag and down he went with it.

"On the bottom George," he said over the phone.

"Right Martin, you are on the bottom," George answered, "go left a bit, about twelve feet to your left." We watched his bubbles travelling along the face of the wall.

"Hold there Martin, you are now directly under the first mark on the quayside," said George. The bubbles now started describing an asterisk as Martin began travelling in and out, all around the central spot he had first stopped at, obviously finding broken stonework and loading it on the bag of explosives.

"Right George that's it, I will come up for the second one, take me away." We gave him the second bag and he went down again and George directed him to its position.

"I don't believe this is happening," said Andrew watching Martin surfacing to take hold of bag number three.

"This job is going too sweetly, I thought he would have fouled it up long before this." George waited until his diver was back on the bottom then began directing him towards the third mark on the quay but when he released the speak switch we found Martin was screaming with rage.

"it to hell the blasted bastard stuff, oh! God Dammit to hell, the blasted bastard stuff." His voice was rising steadily in pitch and constantly repeating the same words.

"Oh! God Dammit to hell the blasted bastard stuff."

George looked over at me with eyes asking the question, what do I do now? as he spread both hands in a gesture of helplessness.

"Oh! The fucking stupid stuff, come loose ya bastard, COME LOOSE YA BASTARD." He roared loudly, as I hurried across to the phone, but before I reached it the outburst suddenly stopped and once more we heard only the gurgling of his bubbles over the phone. I depressed the speak switch and said,

"What the hell was that all about Martin?" This was greeted by complete silence from the diver and George smiled, as if knowing he was back on familiar ground once more as he said,

"He was worried about something, but he has managed to sort it out now." Martin came back on the phone with only a slightly less aggressive voice saying.

"Its alright Bobby, that white stuff got stuck behind my helmet and I could not get it clear so I had to cut it away with my knife."

"What white stuff are you talking about Martin?"

"That white stuff that comes out of the bag."

"You did WHAT?" I asked loudly in both disbelief and horror, at what I was hearing.

"I had to cut it clear with my knife for there was no other way I could free it." said Martin gruffly, as if that was so simple an explanation, that even a child could understand it. Andrew got really excited as he repeated loudly,

"I knew it, I knew it, he will blow us all to Kingdom come, he has cut the Cordtex." I motioned to Andrew to be quiet then asked Martin,

"Do you still have a hold of the bag?"

"Yes of course I still have a hold of the fucking bag," Martin shouted aggressively.

"Martin listen to me, if you lose that bag down there, then my days of diving with the Leith Docks Commission are over, for I am out of here immediately." I was deliberately holding down the speak switch on the phone so he could not interrupt me,

"and if you don't do exactly what I tell you to do, then you and I are finished and one of us is out of this job instantly, now have you got that?"

I released the speak switch and we listened to nothing but the gurgling of his bubbles once again.

"My God you have made him think now," said George.

"Yes and you should have spoken to him like that a long time ago Bobby," said Andrew. Jimmy poked his head out of the cabin door. and said earnestly.
"Andrew is right Bobby you have been too easy-ohsy with him and he needs to be taken down a peg or two for his own good and for the good of everybody else as well." Jimmy was proving he was quite a little Philosopher.

The strained silence over the diver phone continued and I had no idea how Martin was going to react.
"What would happen if he did lose the bag down there?" George asked.
"I really don't know George but there is no way I would ever dream of continuing to dive in the docks with a bag full of Pentonite primars, gelatine dynamite and a short length of cordtex detonating fuse drifting about loose."
"George can I speak to Bobby please," Martin asked in a quiet contrite voice and Andrew immediately repeated the words
"George can I speak to Bobby please," but in a little boy lost voice. I moved to the phone.
"Go ahead Martin," I said.

"Bobby can you just tell me what you want me to do and I will do it right away." The stubborn determination and arrogance had departed from his voice and it seemed as if it was an entirely different man altogether who was speaking to me now.
I told him I wanted him to take the stones back off the number two bag and lay the number three under number two, then load plenty of rocks on the pair of them. That way both bags would fire together for the bag with the cut Cordtex would be triggered by sympathetic detonation.

After this was done, Martin took down number four and completed the job. We pulled out of the way and I left the boat to meet up with the explosive expert. I did not tell him about the stupid mistake my diving buddy had made, although I knew he would become aware of it when he set them off. I stayed beside him as he connected the four Cordtex runs to the detonators and then secured them to his drum of electrical wire. We retired together with him unwinding the drum as we went along.

Now a safe distance away, and with the Harbour Master's permission the explosive man hooked up his box and set them off. He turned to face me afterwards with one quizzical eyebrow raised.

"Two bags went off together, how come?"

I was forced into telling him what had happened and I laughed when he asked.

"What is he, just a young fellow learning the game?"

"No as a matter of fact he is old enough to be my father."

"In that case he is well worth the watching when it comes to explosives," he called after me as I left him.

We netted a fair number of small dead herring and sprats after I returned on board and I remember thinking I no longer had Jonathan to look after, but instead, I now had to turn my attention to the tiny kitten hiding somewhere in our bilges. It had obviously been born to one of the many feral cats running wild about Dockland at that time. Their capacity for survival far outweighed that of domestic cats and they also showed an inordinate fear of the human species, which probably helped them enormously to that end.

After witnessing the damage done to Martin's wrist and thumb, I knew I would have one hell of a job on my hands trying to win the kitten's confidence and save the wee thing's life, but again remembering Jonathan, I had to try.

I realised the infant must have been terrified, cowering in the bilges with the noise of our compressor immediately above it for the duration of the dive, and the sudden blast of the explosives coupled with the previous near drowning experience, then escaping from the hands of a human, all of which would most probably have caused a domestic kitten of that age to expire long before this, nevertheless I had a quiet confidence somehow, that this wee chappie would survive.

Back at our berth Martin could not get ashore quickly enough and rushed off to the diving hut. Andrew came out of the cabin and stood close to me in the stern of the boat and began whispering confidentially,

"If you want to know why you are constantly being warned to keep Buggar lugs out of your magazine ask Spud Murphy." With that Andrew turned back into the cabin leaving me alone with my thoughts in the stern of the boat.

Before going up to the diving hut to fill in my diary, the lads and I set out a plateful of small sprats and a saucer of milk on the floor of the compressor room and then locked the door behind us. There was a big change in Martin after that day and his domineering attitude was subdued for quite a considerable time but it did return eventually, after all the Leopard cannot change his spots.

Unbelievable as it may seem, we saw neither hide nor hair of the young beast over the next fortnight but we found the milk was drunk and the fish were eaten every morning when we would come on board. As time went by we would occasionally catch sight of a pair of tiny blue eyes staring back at us out of the darkness underneath the floating floor that supported our compressor's engine. Then one night I deliberately left no food or milk out overnight.

In the morning I arrived early, opened up the boat and placed a dish of small sprats and a saucer of milk just inside the open door of the compressor room, then retired to the aft end of the cabin and sat down. I felt a deep sadness at the distrust shown towards me as the baby cat crawled flat out on it's belly slowly towards the food and drink. I remained stock still, for I could see it was ready for instant flight if I should move a muscle. I could now see the little beast clearly and I marvelled that such a small creature could have survived what it had been through.

The wide blue eyes never left my face as it quickly devoured the small fish and lapped up the milk then, as if a magician had waved his wand the black and white baby vanished beneath the floating floor once more. Several mornings were to pass by in a similar fashion, before I left the food and drink on the inside of the coaming between the compressor room and the cabin, thus encouraging the reluctant infant to climb over the coaming and into the cabin beside me before reaching the food and drink. Once this was achieved, I concentrated on slowly reducing the distance between us each day, while I spoke quietly and soothingly to the baby.

I was beginning to gain it's trust and when I told Mabel and the girls about her, for she was a baby girl cat, they promptly christened her Pixie and implored me to bring her home to live with us.

It seemed to take forever to gain her trust, for I was not only fighting against the psychological horror the kitten had been through but I had also to overcome that inherited feral fear of the human race.

Thanks initially to Martin's love of animals, which had saved her in the first instance, I eventually won her trust and took her home to Mabel and the girls.

One year later she would climb up on my knee as Mabel, our daughters and I, sat by our coal fire on a cold winter's night and Pixie would purr with contentment to be the latest member of our family.

Chapter 30

The Death of Cousin Dod

The morning I heard my cousin Dod Donaldson had been killed whilst diving with Balfour Beattie at Cockenzie must be rated as one of the worst days of my life. I had trained him as a diver, after he left his long time employment with CHR. Salvesen's of Leith and finally came home with the last of the whaling men from South Georgia in 1962. The tragic news of his death brought all the old memories flooding back.

My mind transported me back over a great number of years, to the time I myself was no more than a boy of twelve years of age, and once again I was talking to an even younger boy than I.
"It just looks like an ordinary field of grass Dod, but see how worried the Plovers are because we are here." Above us the Lapwings circled and performed aerobatics as their broad wings allowed them to wheel and somersault through the air, while their alarm calls rang out periodically. "Pee-wit, Peeeee-wit, Peewit-Peewit."
The bird's concern was palpable to the extreme.

"This field is their home Dod and we must be careful not to step on their nests and smash their eggs."

We had climbed almost to the top of the hill and were now walking in the last of the arable land belonging to Bannatyne Mains Farm, before its cultivated fields gave way to the rolling moors of heather, inhabited only by grouse, curlew, duck and the wild red deer. Later in the year this field would be harvested as hay but at present the new grass was only inches high.

The wee boy's eyes were more often than not turned up at the sky, fearful of the diving birds, rather than searching the ground for nests. This was the third time I had taken him over the same area trying to get him to find a nest of four eggs by himself. Each time he had walked close by them, but his eyes were turned up at the angry diving birds. My repeated advice not to step on any eggs finally worked as he glanced down in front of his feet. The young boy's face lost its concern over the birds above him and instantly became highly animated when his eyes fell on the nest.

"Oh! Look" he cried, running forward and pointing excitedly.

"there's one there, with four eggs in it," at last he had found his first nest.

Dod was six years younger than I was, and in 1943 he had come to live with us in Port Bannatyne, on the Island of Bute and this was the first time I had taken him bird nesting with me. I will never forget the sheer excitement that the six year old showed after finding that first nest with eggs in it. We carried on quartering the field and walking back and forth in systematic drills and soon had a bag full of eggs, which caused the young lad's eyes to gleam with the excitement of it all.

The war was still on and rationing meant everyone was permanently hungry, especially our young age group, for extra food could seldom be bought and a Plover's eggs are about equal in size to Pullet's eggs and Dod could not get home fast enough to get them eaten.

My train of thought now accelerated forward through the years to the nineteen fifties, just before I was called up for National Service in the Royal Navy and my Dad had confessed that Dod was pestering the life out of him because he wanted to become a sailor and he needed Dad to speak for him and get him away to sea. I was at home one day when Dod arrived and again asked my father.
"Uncle Attie, I don't want to be a Blacksmith, is there no chance you could get me away to sea as a sailor."

He had already started serving his time as a Blacksmith with the firm of Menzies, Ship repairers in Leith docks, but through sheer determination he finally managed to wear my old man down. Dad took the fifteen year old in to Leith, to Salvesen's Offices, to meet Captain Jerry Smith a good friend and former shipmate of my old man. The Captain's seafaring days were over at that time and he was now employed by his company as a personnel manager, in sole charge of hiring all the labour required for the Company's whaling fleet and shore station of South Georgia, which operated in Antarctica.

Dod got his wish and turned away from a Blacksmith's anvil and set off for the Antarctic to become a Whaler. Young though he was at fifteen years of age, he became a member of the crew of the whale catcher the "Southern Broom" and spent many years in that cold and forbidding clime, while they hunted the great leviathans of the Southern Ocean.

I found a deep sadness flood through my body as my thoughts returned to the present time briefly, before sliding back into the past once more and recalling an all night trout fishing trip our extended family had gone on a few years before that terrible day. I had set off on a Friday morning to fish the river Tyne at Amisfield cauld, below Haddington, accompanied by my brother Dickie and Dod and his younger brother Terry and our other cousin young George Selvester. In the early afternoon I was beginning to think we had picked the wrong day, with little flurries of sleet and snow blowing in the wind and not one sign of a rising fish anywhere since our arrival on the river. George Selvester came along the bank towards me saying.
"Hey cousin gonny show me how to catch a trout for God's sake."
"What do you mean show you?"
"I mean show me how it's done, I have never caught one in my life and you and your faither would catch a trout in a bloody puddle." I took a look at his rod and the tackle he was using then said.
"For God's sake George you have a hook on here that would hold the Queen Elizabeth at anchor, no self respecting trout would dream of going near that and your cast is far too heavy as well." I stripped off the ridiculous cast and bent on a 3lb. breaking strain nylon leader and a size 18 hook. "There, that's better, try that but personally I think it's too

bleak a day we have chosen, I did not expect the weather to be so cold at this time of the year."

An hour later I came upon him again, standing on the edge of the bank and tugging his rod downwards trying to bring his hook down out of a tree which overhung the river. He did not notice me coming up behind him until I laid my hand on his shoulder. "No George," I said pointing up at his hook embedded in the branches high above the water.
"You are going about it all wrong, they won't go up there for it, you have to land it in the water."
"Ha! Ha! Very fucking funny," he said derisively as his nylon broke and catapulted the remainder back at him. I patiently bent on a new leader and hook for him saying,
"There you go George, now this time, try keeping it in the water."

By 10 o'clock that night the darkness had set in and the late spring night had become unusually cold for that time of the year. Dickie came along the bank shivering,
"What about it Bro, gonny light a fire to warm us up, the whole lot of us are frozen stiff."
"I will light a fire if you and the rest of the lads will search for logs to build it up."
"Where's the best place to light it?" he asked.
I looked around, and my eyes settled on the dim outline of the ruin of an old pump house, close by the weir. It had no roof, but all four stone built walls were complete and a solid stone floor would all act as a heat reservoir, if fed by a large log fire.

"There" I said pointing to the ghostly form of the pump house shrouded in the beginnings of a freezing fog,
"inside there we will have shelter from draughts once I get a good fire going, you get the lads to search for plenty firewood."

I soon had a small fire going, although it was struggling against the damp timber I was forced to use to start with. As I worked on it, I could hear the rest of the lads snapping timber in the nearby woods. Cousin George Selvester came in carrying a bundle of small branches and dropped them on the stone floor beside the rest of the accumulating fire wood.
"God its cold and that's not much of a fire is it?" he asked grinning cheekily at me. I understood my Cousin's sense of humour only too well, for it ran on parallel lines similar to my own.
"It will be, when I get it going properly," I answered,
"and you start bringing me some thicker logs so I can chop into the centre of them and find some dryer wood."
"Oh! I might have guessed it would be my fault the bloody fire won't go properly," George said, whooping with a giggling laugh, like a demented hyena, which reminded me instantly of my Aunt Chattie, his mother's attractive giggle.

Dickie and Terry came in and threw down their contribution to the wood pile, both of them laughing fit to bust their sides,
"Dod just fell out of a tree," Dickie explained.
"What the hell was he doing up a tree? I asked,
"has he hurt himself?"
"He seems to be o.k. but he has hurt his back" Terry answered, still laughing at his older brother's misfortune.

Dod followed them in, grimacing as he held the small of

his back with both hands. I could see he was not very happy at the younger men laughing at him.

"What happened Dod?" I asked.

"I saw a tree with a Y fork about ten feet above the ground and one side of the Y looked rotten so I climbed up and put both feet on the rotten side while my back was against what I thought was the sound side, but when I stamped on it the sound side behind me broke off and down I came."

He glared at Dickie and Terry who could not stop their sniggering.

An hour later we were ringed around a roaring log fire in the centre of the little pump house. The walls were beginning to absorb and bounce the heat back off them, giving a comfortable warmth to our near frozen fishing party. We sat there in silence for some time before Dickie asked if anybody had anything left to eat.

By this time we were more than twelve hours into our fishing trip and all our sandwiches, tea and coffee were long since gone. Nobody had anything left, even the flasks of soup were also finished, having been devoured many hours previously.

"Did you catch anything bro?" Dickie asked hopefully.

"I have one fish," I answered,

"but its not a trout it's a roach"

"Any size is it?"

I reached for my fishing basket and opening it I removed the fish.

"Quite a good fish, as you can see, better than one pound in weight I should say." Dickie's eyes lit up at the sight of the fish.

"Can you cook it so we can eat it?" he said eagerly.
"Yes I can do that" I said, preparing a small roasting tray by weaving some small wet timbers together for the fish to lie on and setting it inches above the edge of the burning embers. George rose up from his place on the other side of the fire. "Well" he announced,
"if you are going to share that one among you, I am going to cook and eat mine all by myself."
"Don't tell me you finally managed to catch a fish." said Dickie, as if George had managed some incredible feat
"Yes earlier tonight I caught my very first ever trout," George said proudly, removing a small 50 gramme tobacco hand rolling tin from his bag and inside its cleaned out interior, there lay a three inch long salmon parr.

"I am going to eat it all by myself, without sharing with anyone, and I will enjoy every mouthful of my first ever catch" George said, while the giggling demented hyena within him laughed loud and long at the sheer idiocy of it all.

After a while I warned the lads that the roach was cooked and ready, but Dickie wanted it well done and well done it was when it finally broke apart and dropped into the fire.

Dickie let out a howl of protest and scooped it out and began frantically scraping off the ash and small embers. They tore into it with gusto, complaining bitterly at the lack of salt to go with it:

Was that happy time only a few years ago, with Dod hale and hearty except for a bruised back and injured ego.

My speed of thought leapt forward in time once more to the year 1962 and the last time Dod and I had worked together.

At that time I was the Chief Diver with the firm of Mitchell Construction Ltd building the dam which recovered the whole of Cockenzie bay from the sea and allowed the present day Power Station to be built there, and the little Fishing village of Cockenzie to more than double its original size.

This was where I trained Dod as a diver, I have already told the whole story in my first book, 'Last of the Hard Hat Divers' so suffice it to say, Dod and I had shared many exciting adventures on that project.

Now, I was devastated at the tragic news of his death and my backward thoughts of more happy days gone by exploded in a kaleidoscope of memories, like confetti scattered at a wedding ceremony and finally culminated in the strange story of the night of the Ettrick Shepherd.

This was supposed to be the fishing trip to end all fishing trips and most of the fishermen male members of our extended family would turn up to go on it. It was early in the same year of 1962 and CHR Salvesen had wound up their whaling business, so cousin Dod was now permanently back home. My father and Uncle George Selvester were the 'Old men' of the group and we all set off in three cars on a Friday afternoon. Our destination was Loch Skein on the flat moorland above the mountain which contained the famous waterfall of the Grey Mare's Tail, whose white water thundered down vertically for hundreds of feet into the valley bottom.

We parked the cars in the empty tourist car parks at the foot of the mountain and laden like pack mules we set off in single file up a very narrow wild goat track which ran up the mountain side to the right of the waterfall. Dod and

Terry Donaldson were in the lead, carrying a large bell tent, which Uncle George Selvester assured us would be big enough for all of us through the night. Next came Dickie and I carrying sleeping bags, camping gear and fishing rods, followed by Dad and Uncle George. The older men carried nothing but their own fishing gear, for the goat track was so steep it gave them enough trouble as it was. Behind them came young George Selvester and his kid brother Irvine carrying ground sheets and more fishing and camping gear.

As we drew closer to the top of the mountain, the slope to the left of the goat track became steeper and alarmingly frightening for it became patently obvious to all of us should anyone lose their footing on the very narrow goat track they would drop hundreds of feet into the chasm cut by the waterfall over millions of years.

It was with a sense of relief we stepped over the summit on to fairly level, heather clad moors.

We now began to head upstream following the large burn which fed the waterfall behind us, and away ahead we could see the water of Loch Skein. The skies above us were overcast, with large volumes of dark clouds piling up all around us but the heather and the moors were dry and the light breeze was pleasantly balmy. Always the optimist at the beginning of every fishing trip I was about to remark on the possibility that the overcast sky might work in our favour, if we fished with large dark coloured flies, when my Dad suddenly said,

"There is a storm brewing so George and I have decided not to stay overnight, in fact we are going to head back down now, while we still have enough light to see our way down that bloody goat track."

"Can I borrow your rod Dad?" Dickie asked

"Yes I will have enough trouble getting down again without carrying anything at all" the old man said. Without another word he and Uncle George turned around and headed back the way we had just come. I was not surprised at Dad turning back, for after all, he was sixty years of age at that time and I was more than surprised he had made the climb in the first place.

After they had gone we carried on to the loch and pitched the bell tent in the heather above the south side. For a few hours the weather conditions remained the same but the fish were reluctant to come to the flies. I then noticed the breeze was backing anti clockwise into the west and gaining in strength and I knew Dad was right, there was a storm coming. I turned back around the head of the loch and made for our camp site. By the time I reached the tent the rain was hammering down and the wind was gusting in powerful blasts.

Everybody was inside and the pump up paraffin stove was snoring loudly when I entered.

"That came up sudden did it no?" said Dod

"Sure did" I agreed,

"and it leaves us with a bit of a problem."

"What's the problem?" asked Dickie and I was about to tell them, when I thought better of it, and decided not to worry the younger members of our party. I had noticed the slack guy ropes were causing the canvas tent to jerk spasmodically as the gusts of wind hit it, at the same time I realised we dare not tighten the guy ropes too much in the driving rain.

"Oh!" I said, quickly altering my answer,

"this probably means the fishing is over for the rest of the night."

"Not much of a problem bro," Dickie answered, "we are nice and comfortable in here and Dod has plenty paraffin for his heater and that's just as well 'cause that wind and rain out there would take the face off you."

Over the next two hours we tucked into fresh sandwiches and hot cups of tea and coffee brewed up on Dod's wonderful little Primus stove which kept the inside of the tent really warm and lit up the interior with a cosy amber glow.

Outside the wind and rain increased in violence and we lay back and listened to it battering our frail canvas walls. After a while I said,

"Have any of you heard of the legend of the Ettrick Shepherd?"

"No who was he?" my brother asked.

"He was a poet by the name of James Hogg who lived about a hundred and fifty years ago and he was also a shepherd who looked after his sheep on the same hills and moors we are on at the moment.

After he died there were many reports from ordinary people who swore they saw his ghost flying across these moors every time the wind would increase to near gale force." Dod gave me a knowing grin, to show he knew I was embarking on one of my ghost stories to frighten the younger lads but he said nothing. I lowered my voice to give more effect to my tale as I continued.

"Over the last hundred odd years or so, the local farmers and other people who lived in this desolate area were wary of heading into these hills whenever the wind would sound like that." I nodded up at the top of the tent which was shuddering under the force of the wind and emitting a mournful wailing, which rose and fell in tune with the individual gusts. I lay back and stared silently at the canvas roof of the tent above me to allow my story to sink into their receptive minds. It was while I lay quiet I became aware I could hear the far off individual blasts long before they reached us and the almost quiet few seconds that lay between them, which prevented it from becoming an all out howling gale. Even although I say it myself, I timed it perfectly as I sat up suddenly and said in a loud voice.

"If it is you out there Ettrick Shepherd, prove it by stopping the wind altogether." With a long sigh the wind died away but already in the distance I could hear it raging across the open moorland and I just had time to shout out loudly.

"I am not convinced, if it really is you, make the wind blow harder than ever." The words were barely out of my mouth before the biggest gust of all hit us and the flapping canvas of the tent screamed like a banshee. I lay back once more and winked at Dod who was grinning at me, as if he too was enjoying the consternation of our young cousins.

About ten minutes went by, with me lying on my back and staring up at the top of the tent, before I realised the canvas fabric was slowly teasing apart under the terrible strain being imposed upon it. I sat upright and yelled

"OK, if it is you James Hogg prove it once and for all by ripping the roof open."

A dreadful tearing sound came from the roof instantly, as if a giant knife had pierced it and was slowly ripping it down towards us. All my young cousins threw themselves face down on the ground sheet howling with fear and Dod roared at me.

"Shut up, for God's sake SHUT UP." and I did.

We gathered in the torn canvas as best we could and hung on to it grimly, rather than be left exposed to the vicious weather on that lonely moor. The bell tent had reduced by about half of its former size and for the rest of the night we were pelted by the incessant rain while hanging on desperately to the torn remnants of the tent.

It was a sorry looking squad that came down fishless from that God forsaken place in the morning. I have often wondered, looking back on that night, whether the uncanny preciseness of all that happened was really due to my febrile imagination alone, or was there some other supernatural intelligence which felt compelled to intervene???

Back to the present time once more, I was anxious to find out the circumstances which brought about the demise of my cousin. I heard it first in Leith Docks from one of our engineers. He told me Dod had been killed by an explosive shot, set off by the Irish firm with the unusual name of Divers, which is pronounced as rhyming with shivers and who were occasionally 'shot blasting' as they were constructing the Outfall Tunnel for the new Power Station at Cockenzie.

David Grieve allowed me to take the day off work, as one of my "Floaters," even although these odd single day holidays were usually only granted when arranged beforehand with our Works Manager. I set off in my car for Cockenzie, armed with my camera and determined to find out who was responsible for my cousin's death. I arrived at Balfour Beattie's offices and asked to see the diving gear that

Dod had been wearing that day. I was told all his gear was in their General Store, so I made my way there and asked the store man to show it to me. He walked away among his many shelves and then came back and laid the remains of Dod's helmet on his counter.

I stared sadly at the buckled helmet. It's front light glass was still clinging in place although completely shattered with star shaped cracks all over it and instead of being see-through glass, it was completely opaque and as white as snow. The back of the helmet was dented inwards and the two elbows of the air hose inlet and the telephone cable had both been ripped clear of almost all of the rivets which secured them to the back of the helmet and bent forward at a crazy angle, buckling the whole back of the helmet violently inwards.

"My God" I said,

"It took some force to do that, the two elbows have almost been ripped off the helmet altogether."

The sympathetic store man nodded solemnly.

"Was he a friend of yours?" he asked and his use of the past tense sent a poignant stab through my chest instantly.

"He was my first cousin and one of the best friends I ever had." The store man nodded understandingly.

"The rest of his gear looks perfectly normal, do you want to see it?"

"Yes I want to take photographs of all the gear he was wearing, before anything goes accidentally missing." I said, adding

"If you know what I mean?"

The store man walked back among his shelves and began systematically loading all Dod's diving gear on the counter, beside the shattered helmet.

One pair of deep water Diving boots, which at first glance seemed to be perfectly normal until I laid them on their side and witnessed at first hand the unusual sight of small pebbles embedded in the underside of their thick lead soles. In all my years of diving I had never seen or heard of anything being embedded in the lead soles of diving boots. I had to have photographs of that, to go with the ones I was taking of the smashed helmet.

Next front and back weights with nothing out of the ordinary about them and finally corselet, brass bands and stud bolts all in good order.

"No suit, no woollens?" I enquired.

"That's all that was brought up here to the stores," said the store keeper,

"the lads who brought up the gear just said the diver was whisked away the moment the ambulance arrived, so they probably took him away wearing his woollens and his suit."

"Did the lads say whether or not they noticed anything else about the state of the diver before they took him away?" I asked

"Yes they said he was completely unconscious when they brought him up."

I stared hard at the store man, as a slim glimmer of hope lanced through my mind.

"Unconscious," I repeated,

"you said unconscious just now, you mean he was still ALIVE when they got him to the surface?"

"Oh! Yes, and he was still alive when he left here, according to the Ambulance men who took him away."

I shot round to Balfour's Offices and a couple of phone calls later I had it confirmed that Dod was still alive, although clinging to life by a mere thread. I returned to the Stores and looking at the helmet again, I began taking more photographs of it from all angles and at the same time I tried to work out in my own head how anyone could have come out of such a crumpled mess alive.

I began by comparing what happened to Dod with my own experience at the Cofferdam at Portobello. I had gone down one day to carry on caulking the clutches with Denso Chord after the Dam began leaking quite heavily and unknown to us at that time a small group of divers were working between Musselburgh and Portobello on another outfall tunnel.

They fired off a shot while I was on the bottom, but the wall of the Cofferdam was between me and the explosion and the wall absorbed most of the shock wave. I was, however, also hauled up to the surface unconscious but neither I nor my helmet suffered any real lasting damage.
Satisfied I had enough pictures of the mangled helmet, I carried on down to the sea front and there saw a heavy duty pontoon diving raft anchored well out beyond the piling of the dam we had built.

A small dinghy took me out to it and there I met one of Dod's diving linesmen. The young man appeared to be still in a state of shock as I asked.
"What happened laddie?" He was sitting on a roughly built bench used as a dressing stool, inside a make shift shelter on the raft and he was struggling with some kind of personal

emotion. He looked up at me round eyed with a bewildered expression on his face as I repeated the question.
"What happened laddie?"

"When we got Dod dressed that morning he went down and he was working away when one of Divers's men came over and told us to bring him up because they were going to fire a shot in the tunnel below him, so we brought him up." He stopped talking and leaned forward, cupping his face in both hands in despair.
"And," I said, prompting him to continue with his story. He straightened up and dropped his hands on his knees.
"Dod sat here fully dressed for hours but nothing happened, then one of the piling crew came aboard and said they had lost a set of guides over the side and could Dod find it for them. He told the man he would, as soon as Divers had fired their shot."

Once more he stopped his story and I waited patiently to allow him to compose himself, then after a while I prodded him on again by saying,
"AND" more forcibly than before. He looked up at me as if I was torturing him, by forcing him to relive the tragic details.
"Divers's man came back and told us they were postponing the shot until tomorrow so Dod went down and he was searching for the piling guides when they fired the shot."

I felt one almighty rage building up inside me. They had told him they were postponing the shot until the following day, otherwise Dod would NEVER have gone down. Sheer negligence, I thought, and a blatant disregard of the safety rules of shot firing, and I resolved there and then I would make them pay for their carelessness, whether Dod lived or died.

Many weeks were to go by before Dod clawed his way back to a semblance of health, but many years would also go by while he still retained the roseate colour of high blood pressure permantly on his face. He was left as a young man with a condition which ensured he would never again find a diving Doctor who would sign his fitness register and as a result, he would never dive again.

I persuaded him to have a meeting with my lawyer Bill Brydon of Nightingale and Bell of No 5 Alva Street in the West End of Edinburgh and make a claim against the firm of Divers and this he did. He had a cast iron case according to Bill Brydon who had gathered a plethora of witnesses willing to swear a true account of what had taken place and armed with my photos and testimony, Bill was cofident he would get Dod a sizeable settlement out of court.

Six months went by and Dod was given Bill Brydon's bill for services rendered to date. This angered him because, being unemployed, he was finding it hard to make ends meet and since he had an inbuilt distrust of lawyers to begin with, he called off the case and allowed the Irish firm to get off Scot free. I felt a real sadness over the outcome, because I was sure under the circumstances he would have won his case and been awarded a worthwhile sum of money, whereas my advice, coupled with Dod's own obdurate nature had cost him a pretty penny instead.

When he and I talked over the events of that day I said.
"When it happened to me at Portobello I knew very little about it Dod, one minute I was Caulking away at the

clutches of the Dam and the next I was coming to my senses flat out on the floor of our diving D K W. I was saved by the wall of the Cofferdam, what do you think saved you?"

Dod gave me his well known crooked grin which caused white streaks to curve around his mouth as the stretched skin etched into the perpetual redness of his face.
"I was lying down on my belly feeling all around me looking for the Piling Guides 'cos I could not see a bloody thing in front of me, when I suddenly felt a terrific pain in the soles of my feet and I woke up in Hospital. I can tell you cous' I never heard a thing nor felt anything other than that quick pain in my feet before the lights went out, but I think if I had been standing up I would have been killed."

I realised Dod had summed it up perfectly, for the shock wave must have slammed into the thick lead soles of his boots, then travelled over his back and smashed into the back of his helmet, almost ripping off the two elbows and as they were cranked violently forward they had crushed the metal inwards forming the huge dent in the back of the helmet. There was no doubt in my mind that Dod was right and if he had been standing upright he would have been killed instantly.

The whole unfortunate incident taught me a valuable lesson that would remain with me for ever. I will never forget how I felt when I was first told Dod was dead. From that day onwards I have never accepted first reports as being the Gospel truth and instead, I am wary of trusting second or third hand stories at any time. Hearsay has a tendency to grow arms and legs as it passes from mouth to mouth until, sometimes, the final outcome becomes a monstrosity of a stranger to the truth.

Cousin Dod died a natural death, finally passing away forty years later, around about 2005 and once again, while writing these memoirs, I have occasionally experienced a strong, eerie feeling that some supernatural power was not only helping me with my writing, but was also correcting some minor mistakes and omissions I was making to begin with, all of which makes a world of a difference to a true life story.

My diving diaries have now reminded me my narrative is fast approaching the end of my time with the Leith Docks Commission. This venerable old Company would shortly become The Forth Ports Authority and the changeover would breathe new life into the Port of Leith, proving the old adage 'All is change or decay' to be correct once more.

I continued diving with the newly formed Company for a further ten years, during which both Martin and I would share many adventures, both laughable and at times sinister. It would also be some time before I would find the answer to my question, why I must never allow him to enter my explosive magazine.

Martin Bendicks was the most complex character of manhood I ever met throughout the whole of my life. I used to pride myself I could very quickly categorize any person's nature after meeting them once or twice but Martin became the exception that proved the rule. He appeared to stand in an indefinable category by himself, which I felt would have defeated the best efforts of the most distinguished Psychiatrists to unravel and try to explain.

Both of us would occasionally rub shoulders with the Grim Reaper himself throughout these final years and sometimes Lady Luck would come to our aid when other peoples mistakes would bring us within a hairs breadth of his poised scythe, but we would both survive his best attempts to remove us from the land of the living and allow me to tell the story in my final book, 'Last of the Hard Hat Divers 3.